A Mother's Side of War

Diana Mankin Phelps

AuthorHouse™
1663 Liberty Drive
Bloomington, IN 47403
www.authorhouse.com
Phone: 1-800-839-8640

Published by AuthorHouse 9/10/2013

ISBN: 978-1-4918-1678-3 (sc)
ISBN: 978-1-4918-1677-6 (hc)
ISBN: 978-1-4918-1676-9 (e)

Library of Congress Control Number: 2013916372

Any people depicted in stock imagery provided by Thinkstock are models,
and such images are being used for illustrative purposes only.
Certain stock imagery © Thinkstock.

This book is printed on acid-free paper.

Because of the dynamic nature of the Internet, any web addresses or links contained in
this book may have changed since publication and may no longer be valid. The views
expressed in this work are solely those of the author and do not necessarily reflect the
views of the publisher, and the publisher hereby disclaims any responsibility for them.

You may not end up
where you expected,
dreamed or planned
you would be.

But, by the Grace of God,
you will always end up
exactly where you are
Meant to be...

In trying to decide who or what to dedicate this book to, I considered many people and many things.

I of course considered my son, my husband, my family and so many others who were not only supportive but instrumental in making this book a reality.

But all these people, in no way would want to take away from the purpose behind the writing of it.

Therefore I dedicate this book to **YOU,**

the American citizens who rose up and answered the call to support and increase awareness, in any way possible, for the benefit of our Military personnel and their families.

A portion of the proceeds from *A Mother's Side of War* will be donated to veterans support organizations.

Table of Contents

Forward

Cpl. Aaron P. Mankin
United States Marine Corps (ret.)

I enlisted in the Marines in 2003. I didn't feel like my family enlisted too, but the day I was wounded by a roadside bomb, I felt like they were drafted. I chose to fight. All they did was choose to answer a phone call; a call every parent hopes they never have to answer; a call every warrior prays their loved ones never have to hear.

Being a combat wounded Marine, I've had to get used to people calling me a hero and asking to hear my story. My story of the war is just one side of things. War has many sides. And in the pursuit of understanding war, it's necessary to know about as many of those sides as possible. This book is about another side of war; a mother's side of war.

My mom and I go way back; farther than even I can remember, since day one, I'm told. While I cannot recall all of our times together like she can, I can never forget how she has always been there for me.

On my first day of school I got so upset I started to cry. Mom leaned over and took my hand. Then she kissed it. Her lipstick left a stamp and she told me this way she would be with me all day. It comforted me and I went to class. We carried on this tradition throughout the over 60 surgeries I've endured. Before I would leave for the operating room, she would kiss me...every time. She never missed a surgery. She was always there, comforting me.

Since my mom answered the call, she has been serving her country by caring for a wounded service member, her Marine and baby boy. She became a nurse, a physical therapist, an engineer, a chef, a valet, a confidant, a coach, a cheerleader, a shoulder to cry on and a witness to more of my recovery than I was.

Just as I will always be a *Marine,* she will always be a *Marine Mom.*

The Phone call

Aaron surprised me with a large bouquet of flowers and a card from the other side of the world. It was Mother's Day, May 8th, 2005, and with him in Iraq the joy of this gift was overwhelming. I missed him so much and worried even more. My other two children, Jason and Sarah, lived close by and had called with their love and wishes for a happy day.

Aaron being so far away made this day a little more difficult. The message on the card made my heart skip a beat and brought a tear to my eye. I put the card in a safe place; where I could pull it out and read it over and over again. It was my connection, and I held it as if I were holding him:

> Mom—Thank you for loving me.
> I wouldn't be the man I am
> without you. I love you and
> I'll see you soon.
> Your Favorite

Mother's Day is a two edged sword for me. The joy my three children bring me is boundless. But, the memory of the child who passed so long ago, at the age of two months, is heavy on my heart. I miss not having the chance to know her and it haunts me on these occasions, more than others.

Three days later, on Wednesday night, my cell phone rang. Because of the hour fear began to grip my heart. I looked at the caller ID and saw it was my ex-husband. Then I was really scared! I knew he could only be calling with bad news concerning Aaron, our youngest son. I did not want to answer that phone!!!

After several rings I picked up the phone, and heard Steve on the other end. His words began very slowly and business like, the same way his father did when faced with a crises. When he said, "Diana, Aaron's been hurt," I started yelling into the phone for him to stop talking. I asked him to tell Don, my husband, because I could not bear to hear this over the phone.

I came rushing out of the bedroom and toward the kitchen, calling out to Don. He met me halfway, asking what was wrong as I shoved the cell phone into his hands telling him it was Steve. He looked at me puzzled, waiting for me to finish my explanation, as I informed him Aaron had been hurt.

Don held the phone up to his ear and turned away listening, as I ran back to the bedroom and fell flat on my face. I was sobbing and praying with my face in the carpet, when I felt The Lord overwhelm me with his presence. I was completely assured He would not take another child from me, and He would be with me through everything still to come…

Don sat me down and began explaining what Steve had told him. There wasn't a lot of information yet. But, they would keep us informed as to Aaron's condition and where he was on his move back to the states. I don't know how I would have survived the heartache ahead without Don to lean on. All we could do now was wait for the next call. I'm not very good at waiting, especially when it comes to my children…

This is what we learned about what happened on that day in Iraq over time, years in fact. When Aaron arrived in Iraq he was assigned to the Public Affairs office in Fallujah. Along with his assignments of writing, interviews and shooting video, he was used as a "model" in some features. Aaron would be referred to as having "Hollywood good looks."

On May 11, 2005, day five of Operation Matador near Al Qaim, Iraq, a massive IED (Improvised Explosive Devise) planted in the dirt road, exploded as the AAV (Amphibious Assault Vehicle) Aaron and seventeen other Marines were in, rolled over it. The blast ruptured the fuel tanks and tossed the twenty-six ton vehicle ten feet into the air. They were less than a mile from the Syrian border about to search a village when the AAV exploded. Six died and all were injured from the flames and searing heat. The black smoke filled the inside as the ammunition began to "cook off" causing addition danger.

As a combat correspondent assigned to II Marine Expeditionary Force, Marine Headquarters Group, Public Affairs Office Headquarters, Aaron was assigned to cover Operation Matador as they headed to western Al Anbar Province, along the Syrian border. Aaron's job was to take pictures, shoot video and write stories. When the IED went off, Aaron was standing up with his camera rolling.

The force of the explosion knocked him to the floor of the vehicle and slammed shut the, now warped, hatch where he had been standing. Aaron remembers everything. The intense heat, the flames engulfing his sleeves and flight jacket, the sound of ammunition exploding, even the cries of his fellow Marines. These are the nightmares that can never be forgotten...

This is the AAV Aaron and seventeen others were in; as it hit the ground engulfed in flames.

Aaron's first reaction was to gasp for air. This allowed the debris, smoke and heat to damage his nose, mouth, and throat as well as his lungs. The back hatch was blown out; Aaron dove for it and realized he was still on fire. When he hit the ground his first instinct was to "Stop, Drop and Roll." Aaron rolled and rolled until he was exhausted to the point of giving up, and made peace with his maker...

The next sound Aaron heard was of his fellow Marines yelling to put him out. They began kicking dirt on him and the surrounding brush. He had on his goggles, so his eyes were saved from the heat, but his face would begin to show the damage done in a matter of days. Aaron had severe burns on both arms and hands. When the fire was out he tried to stand up to help the others still trapped inside, but one of the Marines stopped him. A navy corpsman was there in an instant and placed Aaron on the ground to evaluate his condition, and then ordered him to stay down.

The convoy was close to a school, so the US Army H-60 cas-evac helicopters were landing in the soccer field. Aaron remembers when he was placed on a gurney and carried to the "Bird," he was dropped several times in the freshly tilled dirt. One of the Army pilots said he remembered Aaron because he could smell his burnt flesh in the cockpit. As they lifted off Aaron watched the white, puffy clouds. He thought, "I'm going to die here. This is it." But God had a lot more for this child of mine; more than he could have ever imagined...

Aaron was loaded onto the first helicopter along with three others.

Putting all these "facts" on paper, and looking at these pictures, is one of the hardest things I've ever been led to do...

Note: The reason I use three punctuation marks after some sentences is to remind me of the presence of The Father, Son and Holy Ghost...

I will also use the initials G.I. which refers to "God-Incident." Moments of time, that years later I could see the hand of God guiding us toward His purpose.

After the First Call

After the initial call, the Marine liaison kept us informed with every move of Aaron's journey back home. We were informed he would arrive in Germany at a certain time from the field hospital. Then I received word, a doctor from San Antonio would fly over to Germany and accompany Aaron on the trip back. This plan would have Aaron arriving in San Antonio at Brooke Army Medical Center (BAMC) on Sunday.

Aaron was injured on a Wednesday. Because he was a world away, everything here was being played out nearly a day later. The information we were receiving on Thursday was less than a day old. This plan to get Aaron to BAMC would have him arriving 72 hours after he had been injured.

It seemed like forever as the time dragged on; waiting, waiting and more waiting. I couldn't help but look back on the times when I had come so close to losing both my sons, and the loss of my daughter, Amanda Lee...

Jason was three when Amanda was born. He worshiped her and was so attentive to her every move. She slept through the night from the day we brought her home.

When I entered her room one morning and found her in her crib, so still, gone from what we would be told was SIDS, I crumpled into a deep depression that would be nearly impossible to overcome. The loss of Amanda at the age of two months was truly unbearable.

A little more than a year later, I would be faced with the possible loss of Jason. While eating at a fried chicken restaurant, he had swallowed a piece of bone which lodged in his esophagus. He stopped breathing for an instant and was rushed to the hospital. Because his stomach was full, the doctor didn't want to risk putting him under for surgery until the next morning. Then, they would go through his mouth and remove the bone.

Jason was fairly comfortable through the night; he just felt as though he had something stuck in his throat. He slept until they came in to prep him for surgery, which consisted of putting in an IV. For a five year old, this was extremely traumatic. As he screamed, I panicked. Finally, the IV was in and I kissed Jason as he was taken through those double doors.

When the surgery was over, the doctor called me on the phone in Jason's room with his report. He said the bone had scratched the wall of the esophagus to the point of almost perforating it. It still could very well tear open and if that happened, Jason would be rushed back into surgery and his chest opened. The doctor told me, he probably would not survive an emergency surgery of this kind. The next 24 hours would be crucial.

I was seven months pregnant when this took place. I had lost one child and was faced with the loss of another, while carrying one more. I cannot put into words all the emotions going through me, as I sat by his bed in that hospital room...

By the next morning, Jason was sitting up watching cartoons and eating gelatin. He made it through the night and the doctor released him, with instructions he only be given gelatin for the next week...

Sixteen months after Amanda passed, Sarah Michelle was born. What a blessing to have another perfect and beautiful daughter. Jason's spirit had been renewed as was mine, with her coming. He adored her and watched after her constantly.

Jason and Sarah

Aaron Patrick was born two weeks before Sarah's second birthday. We would celebrate her two year and his two week birthday on the same day. The night he was born was almost his last as well.

On Saturday, January 9, 1982, I was not feeling well. It was still a couple of weeks before my due date and I didn't feel as though I was in labor, I just felt strange. So, we headed to Washington Regional Hospital in Fayetteville, Arkansas, just to check things out.

It turned out when the RN examined me upon my arrival, she felt Aaron's feet through my dilated cervix. This child was not only breech, his feet were presenting first. My water had not broken and I was told if it did, to let them know immediately. The RN who was examining me decided it would be best if she continued to put pressure on the membrane to keep it from rupturing. We stayed in this position until I was in the delivery room, prepped for an emergency C-Section, with my doctor and the anesthesiologist ready to begin.

The danger was Aaron's feet were coming first. If my water broke his feet would slip through the birth canal, along with the umbilical cord, shutting off his oxygen supply and suffocating him. I literally held my breath as I prayed he would not kick. Thank God he was calm the whole time all this was happening.

I asked for an epidural, so I could be awake. I had never missed the first cry of one of my baby's before. The doctor told me it would be too dangerous. As soon as my muscles were relaxed, from any anesthesia, my baby's feet and umbilical cord would slip out. He would only need two or three minutes to deliver him safely. Putting me under, just as the doctor was ready to cut, was the safest way to deliver this child of mine, who seemed intent on entering this world with his feet on the ground.

The day Aaron Patrick Mankin was born was just the beginning of what would be a lifelong fight to keep him safe. He weighed 5 pounds and 15 ounces at birth, yet at two weeks he was still below his birth weight. Our Pediatrician believed Aaron wasn't strong enough to eat a sufficient amount at each feeding for him to thrive. He was eating every hour, but would become too tired before eating enough to be full, only enough to satisfy his hunger. It was decided to put him on a preemie bottle to make it easier for him to get a larger amount of milk with less effort.

This was a solution and a major problem. Aaron was able to take three ounces at one feeding and began to gain weight. But, he was allergic to every formula known to mankind. We tried everything, but they all had side effects. It finally came to the point of, *which one caused the least severe reaction?*

After three months of listening to Aaron's lungs rattle as if he had pneumonia, his doctor decided to take him off formula all together. He put Aaron on Gatorade and baby food. Aaron was also allergic to orange juice, vitamin C supplements and calcium supplements from every source we could find.

I kept thinking Aaron would outgrow some of the sensitivity with each month that past, but he did not. Every time I laid him down at night, listening to his labored breathing and the rattle in his lungs, fear would flood my soul. I was so afraid of losing him during the night I often stayed in his room, listening for each breath he took.

My mind comes back to the present and I wonder if Aaron is on a respirator, or if he is not in need of one. I was waiting anxiously for the next phone call to let me know about Aaron's condition, even though I knew I would not hear anything until he was on his way to San Antonio.

The Lord had already assured me He would not take Aaron's life, so the thought of getting that phone call wasn't even in me…

Unexpected Arrival

Expecting to hear on Saturday afternoon that Aaron was on his way, late Friday night I received word Aaron was in San Antonio and in surgery. This put the time line at 48 hours from injured to BAMC, instead of the 72 hours we had anticipated. Apparently, God had a plan of his own…

A pilot and doctor just happened to be in Germany and called Dr. Renz, at BAMC, to ask if they could fly *"this kid"* over as soon as possible. With permission to fly, they got Aaron from filming the convoy out of the top of the AAV he was riding in, to the best Intensive Care Burn Unit in this country in only 48 hours. (G.I.)

As soon as I was notified Aaron was at BAMC I called Jason, asking him to drive with me to San Antonio. Don was unable to go at once due to medical reasons. Jason had been ready from the time I first let him know his brother was injured. He had been waiting for my call and was ready to travel as soon as I was.

I threw some things in my suitcases, not thinking what I was putting in them. The only important things to pack were my medications. Having Lupus, and all the other diseases associated with it, these meds were the only things keeping me going. I couldn't think of anything other than getting on the road. Whatever I needed could be taken care of later. Don would bring what I had not thought of when he came down.

From Oklahoma City we figured it would take us 7½ hours to get to BAMC. I called my mother, Veda Addington Lindsey, to let her know of Aaron's arrival back in the states. She got on the phone to make arrangements for us to stay on Base. Aaron had never gotten around to sending me the information on what to do or who to contact in case of an emergency, while he was deployed overseas. I was completely in the dark, but all I could think of was getting to Aaron as fast as possible. My child needed me and I needed to be with him…

Mom was retired from the Navy Base just outside of McAlester, Oklahoma. One of her responsibilities had been to make all the travel arrangements for the officers. Her experience with military personnel was invaluable to me. She would make the arrangements for our room on base and would call me as we were driving with the information we needed. (G.I.)

I picked Jason up at his home in Oklahoma City and we hit I-35 and headed south. My mind was numb; I felt as if I were deep within a foggy dream with everything moving in slow motion, and I could not wake from it. I couldn't quite get my senses to sort through everything that was happening.

Whenever I was faced with a challenge, good or bad, my instincts would kick in with logic. I would go to the, "What steps do we need to take, to solve whatever it is, so all could continue in the way required," part of me. The "emotional" part to be dealt with was pushed down and ignored, so I could do what needed to be done to make it all "OK."

As we began the trip, I found myself drifting back in my own thoughts as Jason was continuing to talk as though I were listening. I had so many things running through my mind.

I thought about when Aaron and all of us were in the family room, taking pictures in front of the fireplace, before he left for Camp Lejeune. He would be deployed to Iraq in a matter of weeks.

Aaron took pictures with his sister, Sarah and her daughter Calie, as well as with Don and me. Aaron's brother Jason, and then my sister and her husband had their pictures taken with the handsome, proud Marine.

I needed one of just Aaron and myself...

I held on to him as long and hard as possible. I didn't know when I would see him again...

Before Aaron left for Iraq, he promised he would only be gone for six months. He would be writing for the Public Affairs Office and would be in a "non-combative" area.

I soon learned that every Marine is a rifleman. But, the primary job of a combat correspondent is to tell the story of the war as it unfolds, Aaron was an infantryman when he needed to be. So believing he was not in harm's way was pure ignorance on my part.

I received an email shortly after he arrived in Iraq. I think it was the children that concerned Aaron more than anything. He would have laughter in his voice when he spoke of them.

This picture was attached to the e-mail and he explained it was taken at the Black Water Bridge, a very dark place in the memory of our country.

When he called me a few days later, Aaron talked about how emotional this was for him. He imagined our countrymen as they were attacked by the crowd, and later their bodies were hung on this bridge.

A couple of weeks later, Jason was with a friend of his and pulled out the picture of his little brother. He talked to Tony Benson about how proud he was of Aaron becoming a Marine.

Jason turned his head and saw Tony concentrating on the picture as he sketched. He would give it to Jason and do another one for Aaron, after he had been injured.

Thank you Tony, for this wonderful sketch and the honor you showed in drawing it.

Once Aaron got over there, he quickly changed his status and extended his stay to twelve months. When he called and told me this I said, "I understand, but I don't have to like it." Aaron just chuckled, an extremely strong Marine chuckle, and then replied back, "Oh, Mom."

Then another email came...

Dear Family,

Overall things are safe where I am. There is always a threat and we as Marines are diligent to deny complacency and remain ever ready... Old Glory flies strong in the Middle Eastern winds above our Motor Pool here.

Everyone knows their role. I'm here to tell the stories of the men and women serving their nation.

I'm extending my tour to one year. I want to be here. I need to be here.

Love you all and can't wait to see you again.

"This is it"

End of e-mail.

We had been driving for a couple of hours when Jason interrupted my thoughts, as he suggested we stop for gas and a snack. After a quick break, we were back on the road. Jason continued to talk as I fell back into my own thoughts of the past, not only of Aaron but of all my children...

Reminiscing as We Drive

Jason talked for seven hours straight without taking a breath. I wasn't sure if this was his way of coping with the situation, or if he was trying to keep my mind off of what we might find when we got to Aaron.

About three hours into our trip, my cell phone rang. It was Cindy, Aaron's father's sister. After being married to Steve for 18 years, it was hard for me to think of Cindy as anything other than my sister. She began talking, in a way of preparing me for what was going to happen when I got to Aaron. Her husband, Mike Marvin, had retired from the Air Force at the rank of Chief Master Sargent after 34 years. I kept telling Cindy I loved her. I said it over and over again but she would not respond back to me, and I started crying as we hung up. I know Cindy's heart and I know she loves me, why else would she have called…

When Aaron joined the Marine's it was a difficult decision. However, he had done his research. He knew he wanted to be a combat correspondent and work with the Public Affairs Office, he felt he had a chance at this highly coveted assignment. Aaron was thrilled when he was accepted to the school in Maryland, after Boot Camp, for training to become a combat correspondent. Aaron's high school achievements had made his dreams a reality.

In 1999, Aaron had become the Arkansas Debate Champion at the age of 17. This honor included multiple awards for public speaking and led to his becoming the first student in the history of Arkansas forensics to qualify for national level debate competitions.

As a senior, his entries for the Arkansas Association of Instructional Media's statewide competition in the photography and videography categories won him nine awards, sweeping two divisions and placing first, four times. In 2000, Aaron graduated with Honors. After the ceremony, he walked me to my car where I gave him a diamond ring. I explained the meaning of the circle, to remind him that his path would forever continue. The diamonds stood for the strength of his convictions and faith as this new chapter of his life began. I was so proud of this young man, standing there with tears in his eyes, my Aaron.

High school had not been all work for Aaron. When he was a junior, he was chosen as Mr. GQ. He was entered as "Mr. Debate" and sported a costume, complete with cape, for part of the competition.

This picture would become my vision of Aaron for the rest of his life. Always putting one foot in front of the other, no matter what may come. How could I have known how difficult this would become, in just a few very short years???

Before Aaron left for boot camp in San Diego, he put his arms around me as we talked while sitting on the loveseat. Aaron spoke about how hard it would be for him to be away during the holidays. It was hard for me as well, thinking about Thanksgiving and Christmas without him.

I had become the family cook for these gatherings as my parents had grown older. I was the keeper of the famous "Cornbread Dressing" recipe, handed down from mother to mother. Aaron always looked forward to all the food and fun which was a part of the holiday celebrations.

I would miss his smart remarks and kidding around as well as his loud voice of football opinions flying through the air. Most of all, I would miss his hugs and kisses when he would sneak up behind me in the kitchen.

I had to keep a strong look on my face so he could not see the tears I was holding back at the thought of the upcoming holidays.

Just as Aaron had said, I received this poem two days before Christmas.

Boot Camp Christmas

My face you will not see
And my voice you will not hear.
So these words that you read
Will be my gift to you this year.

Christmas isn't what you make it
It's what it's always been.
A chance for sweet reflection
And forgiveness of our sin.

Presents they surround us,
And not just beneath the tree.
Because I realize my family
Is the biggest gift to me.

I look around my squad bay,
Recruits, to each his own.
If you looked at their Christmas lists
On each one you would find "Home".

My days they stay so busy.
You think it wouldn't cross my mind.
Yet, constant thoughts of all of you
I somehow always find.

I'm here and not alone.
My new brothers keep me warm.
A new memory is earned
On this distant Christmas morn.

I think about the milk and cookies
And about the restless sleep.
But memories of love and laughter
Are the only ones I keep.

I'm not sure how to end this
There's so much left to say.
But I guess I'd better send it off
And pray it finds your way.

Merry Christmas to you all.
My love I will not hide
I miss you all so very much.
I'll see you on the other side.

Aaron Mankin, Dec 2003

As we continued our conversation on the loveseat that day, Aaron looked me in the eyes and told me he would not have the courage to go if not for the trip he had taken to China when he was nineteen. It was a missionary trip with people he had never met, but would soon call brothers.

This picture is the only time Aaron had allowed his hair to grow out. He sported this same hairstyle as a four-month-old infant. The curls hanging loosely around his face and down the back of his neck were a delight to see. However, I was getting tired of other people telling me how cute she was.

So I took him to Gary's Barber Shop, and while I held his head up, Aaron got a "Boy's" haircut. He looked like a little man. When Aaron was two months old, I was combing his hair to the side. But, by the time he was four months old the curls were everywhere and his bangs were hanging in his eyes.

In China, three of the volunteers would leave the compound and hike, camp and eat whatever they had.

They would visit small villages and leave scriptures, in the native languages, under rocks or bushes. The three weeks he was there, he could be seen wearing his Superman neck chain. Before he left for Iraq, Aaron put this chain around my neck and asked me to keep it for him until he returned.

There, on my neck it would stay for several years…

I turned my head to look at Jason as he continued to talk. I had no idea what he was saying now; I just nodded as though I had been listening. We passed a sign showing we were 60 miles from San Antonio, we were almost there...

I slipped back into my thoughts as Jason continued to talk. There had been too many times, in Aaron's life, when I had come so close to losing him...

Fighting for Aaron

Jason had started a new story; I guess he was getting as anxious as I was, as we grew closer to San Antonio. I watched the mile markers go by one by one, it seemed as though we would never reach Aaron. I had been told the surgery would take hours. He should be out by now. I needed so much to be there with him.

I have never left a child of mine alone in a hospital. I stayed with each of my children every time they were hospitalized, night and day until I could take them home. I had been with Jason, then Sarah and Aaron when they were each in a hospital bed. I had to watch over their care, with my maternal instincts, to make sure they were receiving the proper amount of attention.

As Jason continued with his latest tale, I slipped back to the years of fighting for Aaron's life, time and time again. He had been through so much in his short life, yet would always amaze me with his loving spirit even when he would be gravely ill…

After nearly losing him at birth, when he was ten months old, the next threat to try and claim Aaron's life rose up from the depths of Hell…

It was just after Halloween and I picked up some bananas, among other things, from the store on my way home from work. I went by Karen Clark's, my best friend and second mother to all my children, to pick up Sarah and Aaron. As I enter the house through the garage, I had Aaron in my arms as Sarah rushed by me to go find "Bubba." Jason would get off the school bus about 45 minutes before I would get home from work and Karen was just around the corner if he needed anything.

Aaron was so hungry, I pulled a banana out and as I peeled it he leaned over and took a bite. This was unusual; I always pinched off each bite with my fingers and feed each one to him.

As soon as he swallowed the banana, he began to choke and started turning blue as I franticly tried to clear his airway. Finally, I had to make a decision if my baby was going to live. I put my finger in his mouth and pushed it all the way down his throat. This pushed the obstruction into his lungs and cleared his airway. Aaron was breathing, but it was obvious he was having difficulty and I called Karen while still holding him in my arms. Karen's husband was the Director of Respiratory Therapy at our hospital and I had been a respiratory therapist in Springfield, Missouri, so we both had an idea of the problems ahead for Aaron.

Karen was at my house in a minute. I was talking to the doctor's answering service as she entered the door. They instructed me to take Aaron to the hospital at once. Karen dropped Sarah and Jason off at her house, to stay with her husband while she drove Aaron and me to the hospital. I called Aaron's father, and he would be at the hospital as soon as possible. Steve arrived shortly after we got there, and Karen left heading for her home to help with Sarah and Jason.

I told the doctor on call, who was a partner with our Pediatrician, what happened and he ordered a breathing treatment to help open up Aaron's airway. The doctor assured us all would be fine, the piece of banana would dissipate and his breathing would be eased very quickly.

When they finished with the treatment, we left and went to Karen's to pick up Sarah and Jason on our way home. Karen and Alan had two children the same ages. Michael and Jason were best friends as were Sarah and Shawna, so they were often together and Michael was a frequent overnight guest in our home.

That night was long and restless. Aaron's breathing was becoming more and more erratic, and by dawn he was covered in a misty sweat. I had been holding him all night, watching, waiting and praying. Every couple of hours Aaron would stop breathing; it was as though he couldn't catch his breath. I would pat him firmly on the back and he would start breathing again. This pattern continued all night and into the morning.

As soon as the doctor's office opened, I called Dr. Harmon. I was still holding Aaron in my arms as he came on the line. I quickly explained what was going on and he asked if that was Aaron he was hearing. I told him it was, and he said to get him to the hospital and be prepared to stay.

Once again we shuffled the kids and headed to the hospital in separate cars, so Steve could leave when things settled down. Dr.

Harmon met us at the Emergency Room and was alarmed at what he was listening to. He ordered more breathing treatments, x-rays and an oxygen tent along with two IV's.

With all the hustling going on, I didn't notice which arm the nurses were placing the IV's. They were in his left arm and taped to a board. This was to prevent Aaron from bending it, but now he couldn't reach the thumb he sucked. I tried to get him to take the other one, but he wasn't having anything to do with that idea. Aaron would just lay there and look at his thumb on the other end of the board, but he never whimpered or cried. He just looked at it, then back at me to fix it. There wasn't anything I could do…

The nurses on the floor quickly fell in love with the sweet, blond headed little boy who hugged. Every time one of the nurses would get a few minutes they would come into Aaron's room, pick him up and take him for a walk down the hall. Most babies get "White Coat Syndrome." This means, when they see someone in white coming toward them, they think that person is coming to inflect pain, so they start crying in anticipation. But not Aaron, he loved everyone he met and went to each of them with a hug.

Aaron's pattern of breathing continued to be problematic all through the night, and into the next morning. The next day Aaron still wasn't showing any signs of improvement, and we were all baffled as to what was causing him to stop breathing. By now pneumonia was settling in his lungs, *but why,* nothing made any sense.

That evening, Steve left and I was watching Aaron for the next attack to occur. Soon it did, and it was a bad one! No matter what I did, he just couldn't catch his breath. I held him close as I ran toward the nurses' station, dragging the IV pole with me. The respiratory therapist was coming down the hall to give him a treatment, and saw me coming. She dropped her equipment and started running toward me. She took Aaron from my arms while disconnecting the IV, and ran down the stairway.

I was just standing there with empty arms, across from the nurses' station while they watched, and tears started to roll down my cheeks. I had no idea where my baby had been taken or if he was still alive. At that moment, the elevator doors opened and there stood Karen. She saw the panic on my face and hurried to me with her arms out, as she asked what was happening. One of the nurses stepped over and told me she heard Aaron cry out in the stairwell. She also told me the therapist had taken him down to the Intensive Care Unit for Preemies. They had the equipment designed for infants that would be needed to resuscitate him and stabilize his breathing.

Karen knew the way, so we headed down the stairs to find Aaron. When we were in the stairwell, Karen told me she had been headed to pick up a stuffed animal for him before she came to visit. But, The Lord told her to go straight to the hospital. Karen was at the exact place, at the exact moment, I needed her to be. (G.I.)

When Karen and I reached the floor where Aaron was we were directed by the nurses to a private waiting room. Almost immediately Dr. Harmon was there, and he called in Dr. Reese, an Ear, Nose and Throat specialist. Dr. Reese had removed Jason's tonsils, two years earlier, so we knew him and he knew us. At some point, Steve arrived and Karen left.

Dr. Reese and Dr. Harmon decided they had to go in and see what was going on in Aaron's lungs and airways. Dr. Reese was direct in explaining the risks involved in doing surgery on a baby with severe breathing difficulties. But we all agreed we had to find out what was causing these episodes.

Within thirty minutes Dr. Harmon came out, still in his full surgical scrubs with a container. In the container was a wood match stick, covered in what appeared to be banana. This had been pulled out of Aaron's upper bronchial air passage by Dr. Reese. The match stick, approximately ¾ of an inch long, had been pushed through the soft skin of the banana, probably as a Halloween prank. That was the day I learned wood doesn't show up on X-Ray's.

When Aaron was out of surgery, and back in my arms I could breathe again. But, the pneumonia was still a major problem to be dealt with now. We spent five more days in the hospital while he was treated with antibiotics and breathing treatments. Finally, I took my baby back home and continued with more antibiotics. This battle would last for almost two years. Every time I thought the fight was over, Aaron would begin to run a fever and the battle was raging once again.

Back to watching the mile markers, I saw we were only thirty miles from San Antonio. Jason suggests we stop and take a break, gas up and get something to drink. I agreed, and the next station was only a mile ahead. It would feel good to stretch my legs and breathe the night air for a minute or two. We were still in a hurry, so the stop didn't last long and we were quickly back on the road.

Jason began to tell another story as soon as we were back on the highway, and once again I started watching the mile markers. We were so close now. It wouldn't be much longer before we arrived at Fort Sam Houston Army Base.

As I drifted away into my thoughts, I tried to count how many times Aaron had worn a cast after breaking a bone. I can't remember how many times he broke a wrist, arm or ankle during his growing up years. I'll never forget his first broken wrist. The phone call from his school had me in a panic, rushing to him and then to the doctor. We sat in the waiting room as Aaron remained calm with the magazine wrapped tightly around his little six year old arm. I hid the tears in my eyes and the lump in my throat as I talked calmly to soothe his fears.

This was only the beginning; I learned never to question it when Aaron would come in and tell me he had broken something. I knew to trust him in knowing what it was. I sometimes thought he was trying to have as many different colors of casts possible. That phone call was so minuet compared to the last one I had received…

Arriving at BAMC

The drive had been long and yet somehow it seemed to pass rather quickly. We were almost there and my heart ached with my every thought of Aaron. Jason and I pulled up to the guard's gate at three on Saturday morning and entered Fort Sam Houston Army Base. With directions from the guards, we went straight to BAMC and up to the Intensive Care Burn Units waiting room.

There was a paper on the table next to a phone, with the number and instructions to call the nurses' station inside the unit. I picked up the phone and dialed, anxiously awaiting a voice to answer. When I identified myself as Aaron's mother, the nurse said she would be right out. She wanted to prepare Jason and me before we went in to see him. She explained he had been out of recovery for over an hour and the room he was in would be very warm. This was to let his body focus on healing, without having to work at regulating his body temperature.

We followed her back to Aaron's room and as we put on the sterile gowns, gloves, and masks, she told us if we felt faint to head for the door and they would help us out to a cooler area. The nurse decided to stay with us, to answer any questions and to make sure we were alright.

I had seen a lot of Intensive Care Units, and Emergency Rooms when I was a respiratory therapist in Springfield, Missouri before moving to Rogers. Whenever a code was called it was my responsibility to respond and provide cardio–pulmonary assistance. My experience in working with respirators gave me an advantage in assessing Aaron's condition, when we finally got back to him.

When I entered Aaron's room I stood just inside the door, watching. The room was large and dimly lit. I looked slowly around the room, trying to take in everything. I listened to the respirator and took a quick inventory of the tubes running in and out of my child's body. From the doorway, I could not see Aaron's face.

I looked at the bed where he was lying. It was different from anything I had ever seen. The bed was the size of his body and no larger. It appeared to have a scooped out middle filled with a waterbed kind of mattress. His head was held on a stand like pillow; it cradled and restricted the movement of his head. Aaron's arms were stretched out on side fixtures attached to the bed. These held them straight out from his shoulders. They had the same appearance as his bed with the waterbed lining, where his bandaged arms rested.

Aaron's arms were bandaged all the way up to his armpits. I thought at the time, the flames had not scorched the hair under his arms; strange thoughts entered my mind at odd moments like this. Each of his fingers and both hands were wrapped in blue tape. I counted his fingers as if he were a newborn, to make sure they were all there.

Aaron's legs were also wrapped in white gauze from his knees to just below his groin area. This was where they had taken skin to graft onto his arms and hands. His arms and legs were the only parts of his body covered with bandages. He had a tube in his throat, where the respirator was connected, and IV fluids were hanging from several poles. The nurses placed a loincloth loosely over Aaron's groin area. He laid there completely bare, from head to toe except for the bandages. No gown or sheet to cover him, only a loincloth. I wondered how Aaron escaped such a forceful explosion without a broken bone. As I looked at Aaron, all I could see was the "Cross." That was the position he was in with his arms outstretched...

Aaron was very swollen, about 2-3 times his normal size. I checked his arms to see if they had been cut down the inside, so they would not burst from the swelling, and saw they had. This procedure is called a Fasciotomy. This is a common practice when the swelling is severe. They had been pumping fluids into him as fast as possible to keep him alive.

I was praying as I looked at the crucifixion, by fire, of my son. I knew this test of Aaron was one allowed by God, for a purpose I could not begin to imagine. I asked myself, and God, "What is in Aaron's future that the need for such a terrible price must be paid?" In the months to come Aaron would comment, "You can't have a testimony, without a test."

I walked quickly now, over to Aaron's bedside and gazed down at my son's face. It was beautiful; there was only a small dark spot on the tip of his nose. The searing heat of the explosion had not yet affected his features. He looked as though he had a deep tan, and appeared to have a reddish sunburn as well. On the tip of his nose, the black spot looked as though someone had touched it with a black marker.

I looked at the respirator and saw he was triggering each breath; it did not have to "kick in" to make him take one. It was continuing each breath he started, ensuring they were fully expanding his lungs, but he was starting them on his own. This was an extremely encouraging sign to me.

I leaned down to his ear and spoke, "Aaron, Momma's here." As my words came out, his heart rate increased and his blood pressure went up. Aaron knew I was with him, now he could rest.

I would repeat this message every time I went in to see him. The nurses were generous in allowing all of his family to see Aaron as often and as long as we wanted. I knew it was important to keep reassuring him I was there. That was my focus, to remind him constantly he was safe.

No matter how frightened I might be, I knew the way I reacted would be the influencing factor in how Aaron would coop with everything to come during this time of recovery. I prayed for a calm spirit to overcome and dwell within me.

Jason was standing about half way between the door and Aaron's bed, just watching. After I had spoken, he realized Aaron could hear us, so then Jason spoke. The same reaction to Jason's voice was seen on the monitors. He repeated over and over, "Aaron you're my Hero man, I love you!"

After an hour or so, the nurse suggested we go check in and get some rest. Jason and I left and went back outside to the car. We just stood there for a minute not wanting to leave, but knowing we should go.

The Powless Guest House was just across the street from the front entrance to BAMC, so we wouldn't be far.

The Powless is a hotel for families of wounded warriors and a place where the out-patients stay while undergoing treatment. The rooms consisted of two beds, one bath, a TV and VCR in a dresser with a side desk, one chair, one recliner, a microwave, under counter refrigerator and sink with a cabinet. A rather small room for two people to live in for months, but we didn't need much.

By 7:00am Jason and I were ready to get back to Aaron and see how he had done during the night. That night consisted of the 2½ hours we had been gone.

My family's response to any crises was to rally around and provide support. My mom and dad arrived shortly after noon. My sister, her husband and their daughter followed a couple of hours later. Sarah was working on getting to San Antonio as soon as she could make plans for the care of her daughter. Everyone took turns going in to see Aaron while the others stood around the halls outside the waiting room.

I went in almost every time someone did. The nurses were good about not putting a head count on us. Sometimes I went in alone. Every time I would go to Aaron I would repeat the same message, "Aaron, Momma's here." I had to keep my focus; I had to make sure he felt safe.

Dr. Renz had been in surgery most of the day, when he came into the hallway where we were all assembled. He asked for the "Decision

Makers" to come with him to a conference room. I took a deep breath and followed him. Dr. Renz showed us some pictures of Aaron's upper airway and vocal cords, before and after being cleaned up in surgery, so we could see the extent of his inhalation injuries. Dr. Renz continued to tell us about all of Aaron's injuries and the plan for his recovery. My family was eager to hear what the doctor had said, when I returned.

The next morning while sitting in the waiting room, a tall man with a truly kind face came over to ask if I was with Aaron Mankin. I told him I was his mother as he sat down beside me and introduced himself. This man would become one of my dearest friends, a father figure and someone I could count on for anything.

Don Oneal had received word of Aaron's arrival and had been the first one to see him the night he arrived in San Antonio. Months later, while Aaron and I were having dinner in his home, he spoke of the night he first saw Aaron. He went home and told his wife, "I don't think that boy is going to make it."

Don was 65 and a retired Marine Master Gunnery Sergeant and former combat correspondent in Vietnam. He lived in San Antonio and was serving as National Chairman of the United States Marine Corps Correspondents Association, a group consisting of active duty and retired Marine reporters and photographers.

Don had been wounded in Vietnam and received a Purple Heart. He shrugs it off and says it was just shrapnel, not anything like this kid is going through, referring to Aaron's injuries.

When Sarah arrived she was anxious to see Aaron as soon as possible. She was unprepared for the warmth of the room. After a few minutes, I noticed she was beginning to slowly sink to the floor. I waved at the nurse outside as I grabbed Sarah and she opened the door and helped me get her out. After a few minutes, with a cool cloth on her face, she was fine and went back in a short time later.

I can only imagine what Sarah and Jason were going through now. When my brother died unexpectedly four years earlier, I was so full of anger as well as regrets for words unspoken and time not spent with him.

When Aaron arrived at BAMC, his best friend, Travis Coursey wanted to get to him as fast as possible. He was one of the first people I talked to after seeing Aaron. I found out a couple of days later he had been told not to come yet. Travis was in such agony over Aaron's injury that he was inconsolable. I didn't understand why he had been told not to come as soon as possible. I went into Aaron's room, to ask if he wanted Travis there. His lips formed the word, "Yes." Travis came.

Travis always came, whenever Aaron needed or wanted him, he was there. The two of them would always "be there" for each other, then and now. I cannot imagine two closer friends. They had been best friends since childhood and always had each other's back as they grew older. Aaron and Travis had shared an apartment after High School and had grown even closer living under the same roof. They were learning what it was like to be on their own and the true meaning of "Friendship." These two will always be...

41

On the third day, one of the nurses came up to me in the hall and whispered Aaron was a little more aware, asking if I wanted to go in by myself. Of course I did, so we went to Aaron's room without alerting anyone of my disappearance.

One of the strongest traits Aaron has always had is his sense of humor. I walked in and went to his bedside and whispered my usual statement of being there. Then I felt he needed more, so I asked him if he knew where he was. I was amazed when he shook his head, ever so slightly, from side to side.

Aaron was opening his eyes, trying to see my face as if to make sure he wasn't dreaming. They were so swollen, and he could only manage a slight squint. After he had replied, with the nod of his head, I leaned in a little closer and whispered, "You're in Texas." Aaron looked up at me, and like a true Arkansas Razorback, he rolled his eyes in utter disgust.

I knew he was going to get through this just like my son did every time he faced any adversity in his life, with faith and humor. I thanked The Lord for that peek into Aaron's resilience and wept quietly, just outside his door. This would be an extremely long journey for us both…

My parents left the next day. When my mother got home she went to her computer and pulled up all the emails that were flooding in. She would be my assistant in the months to come and take charge of checking all the messages coming in and sending out answers and updates in my name. Every night we would talk and she would give me the information about each message. We would then discuss how to answer each one and she would take care of sending them out. Aaron's father had added my name to his email list so I would know what was going on from his side. When mom saw the report he put out, she called me immediately. Everyone on his list had been informed Aaron "might not make it."

Mom wanted to know if the doctor had said anything about Aaron not making it, I responded to her, "Definitely Not!!!" I could hear her on the other end of the phone as she let out a sigh of relief. After a moment, Mom made the suggestion we put out an additional email. We wanted to let people in Iraq, as well as those around us, know things weren't all gloom and doom. We let them know of Aaron's responses to us. We also explained the possibility Aaron might be removed from the respirator in a few days, if he continued to improve as he had been.

<u>Never, ever did anyone tell me, or infer in any way, that Aaron would not "Make It"!!!</u>

I continued to send emails of the positive aspects of Aaron's recovery. By then he had made it through several surgeries and had been taken off the respirator, intermittently. I felt all the people who were so concerned, needed to know Aaron was not only stable but improving.

During the second week, I was in with Aaron and there was a question he wanted to ask. He was about to go into surgery again, but he could not speak with the tube still in his airway. The respirator was still in the corner of the room, but he was breathing on his own without it. He only needed an oxygen mask over the tube, to ensure his oxygen levels were maintained and the moisture helped the healing process in his upper airways.

The nurse was in the room and removed the mask while putting a finger over the tube so he could speak. He asked, "Mom is this (surgery) a set back?" I told him, "No baby, you are doing great. This is just part of the process." He was calmed and gave a slight grin as he relaxed, closed his eyes and the nurse put the oxygen mask back over the tube. I knew he had no idea how long a recovery he would have to endure. By the end of the week, Aaron was doing much better and the tube would be removed soon.

When Don arrived, I was able to lean on him when we were alone. This was when I could just be. I didn't have to be strong or act like I was in control of my emotions. He was my safe place. He never showed his own struggles and was a constant support to me, even though I would be away from home for almost nine months...

Burns

The Nature of the Beast

It is impossible to understand what Aaron was going through without knowing the nature of the beast...

Burns can be minor all the way to life threatening and fatal. You must determine the degree of damage done to the tissue and how deep the damage is, before you can tell the severity of the burn and how it should be treated.

Listed below are descriptions of the first four levels of burns:

> **First-degree burns**. The top layer of the skin will show redness and have minor pain associated with it. Sunburn is a good example of this level of burn and usually clears up in less than a week.

> **Second-degree burns**. Redness, pain and swelling are associated with this level of burn, which affects the top two layers of skin. It may look wet and blisters can occur. There is the possibility of scarring as well.

Third-degree burns. This degree of burn is critical. Anyone suffering this level of burned tissue is in need of immediate emergency care. Burns of this degree are referred to as "Full Thickness Burns." They reach deep in to the fat layer beneath the skin, usually nerves are destroyed and there may not be any pain. If the nerves are not completely destroyed the pain can be severe. The skin may look as though it has a deep tan, or could be white and waxy in appearance.

Fourth-degree burns. This level of burn reaches deep into the muscle and bone structure of the body. The burned area usually has an appearance of blackened skin, and because of the destroyed nerves no pain is felt.

Aaron had sustained some second-degree and mostly third-degree burns on his hands, arms and face, approximately 25% of his body.

When burns cover over 15% of the body, there can be many complications. Aaron had to be watched closely for the ones most likely to affect him.

Life-threatening infections.

Severe blood and fluid loss.

Increased risk of hypothermia or low body temperature.

Breathing difficulties from smoke inhalation.

Bone and joint problems.

All of these complications had to be dealt with in Aaron's case. The top four were life-threatening and had to be address immediately. As soon as he was in a field hospital, IV's were started to keep fluids and antibiotics going throughout his body. The loss of fluids was a major concern and they pushed fluids and blood into him as fast as possible. This would continue for several days and then taper down.

Keeping Aaron's body warm was another concern. The room he was in at BAMC was kept at a higher temperature and humidity level; this allowed Aaron's body to concentrate on the healing process.

Aaron had literally inhaled smoke, debris and intense heat, causing inhalation distress. His voice was a faint whisper which took years to improve and surgery to release scar tissue binding his vocal cords.

When Aaron reached Germany they immediately put him on a respirator to help him breath. The swelling, as well as the inhalation damage, could have easily closed his airway completely.

Another major factor which impairs breathing is an increase of lung water. This is a defense which is triggered by the body when it sustains any kind of major injury. Aaron did not have this severe reaction and was able to maintain breathing with the assistance of a respirator.

The loss of skin on Aaron's hands and arms had to be dealt with as soon as he reached BAMC. The grafting of skin from healthy sites onto the burnt areas would be done over and over again. This made two different sets of injuries for Aaron's body to deal with.

Out of Intensive Care

The day was approaching for Aaron to leave the Intensive Care Burn Unit and move onto the main burn ward. This involved a move from one room to another one down the hall and around the corner.

Now, this may not sound like a very large move since he would still be on the burn ward, but believe me it was a tremendous accomplishment. One day, the only retired Marine on the nursing staff in the Intensive Care Burn Unit, told me they had rarely had Marines in there before. When Aaron arrived she informed the staff to get ready because the Marines were coming, and they did. Throughout the course of the war in Iraq, we would see so many severely wounded warriors come through those doors at BAMC. Most of them went back out…

Aaron had a special visitor the day before he was to be moved. The highest ranking enlisted Marine in the Public Affairs field had flown in from the Pentagon, Master Gunnery Sergeant Al Moore. He had come to BAMC specifically to see Aaron. He was also a very good friend of Don Oneals.

Don, Al and I had lunch the day before Aaron was to be moved, not knowing at the time the doctors were considering moving him. We went to the dining hall in the basement of the hospital and found a place to sit next to several young soldiers. They were being very loud and telling some stories that were not meant to be over heard. The language was colorful if you know what I mean. I leaned over to the soldier sitting on the table next to me, and told him there were two "Gunny's" with me and to please hold it down. The young man said "Cool" and then looked up at Don and Al.

Never before have I seen a whole room full of soldiers change their "direction" as when Al Moore and Don Oneal gave one long, authoritative stare at the men on the other side of me. The soldiers at our table immediately left, trying to hide their names stitched on their uniforms. After lunch we went up to see Aaron, then I went back to my room at the Powless to get some rest. While Al and Don went their way, to catch up as old friends do.

When I went back over to BAMC that afternoon, I was informed they would be moving Aaron from the Intensive Care Burn Unit to the main burn ward, the next morning. Al and Don let me know they both intended on being there, to witness the big move...

I stayed up all night, like a small child waiting for Santa Clause to come down that chimney. This move would allow me to spend an unlimited amount of time with Aaron. The tube in his throat had been taken out a few days earlier, so Aaron would be able to communicate and the wound was closing very quickly. I couldn't wait for the anticipated freedom which this move would give to us, the very next day.

Al, Don and I gathered in the hall outside Aaron's room, anxiously waiting on the signing of all the papers so he could be transferred and begin the next stage of his recovery. When the transport people came into the room, Aaron just shook his head from side to side. He insisted on walking out of there and to his new room. All of us were a bit skeptical, but stood aside as the orderly's helped Aaron to his feet.

The nurses were amazed the first time they got Aaron up in a standing position. They had never seen Aaron standing and did not realized how tall he was while he lay in the hospital bed. One nurse told me later, "He just kept getting taller and taller," as they watched him stand for the first time. Here you can see how Aaron spills over as he takes a quick nap on the couch at my parent's home, after returning from boot camp.

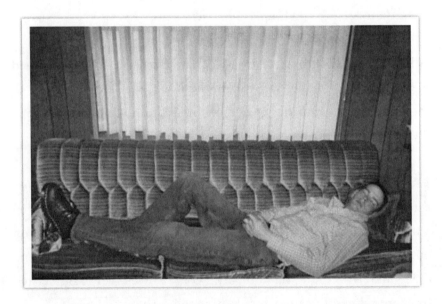

As time went by, before a surgery when a nurse would inquire about his height he would reply "5'12" causing them to scratch out what they had begun to write.

The three of us stood behind as Aaron walked, with an orderly on each side, out of his old room and slowly down the hall toward his new home on the burn ward. About half way down the hall, I noticed Al had fallen a step behind. When I turned and looked at him there were tears running down his face. He hugged me as he sobbed and apologized for getting so emotional. He said his wife was always getting on to him about getting too attached, when it came to the men under his watch, but he just couldn't help it...

Finally, we reached Aaron's new room and the nurses quickly took over getting him settled into his new living quarters. A couple of the Marine Liaison's had come up to see how Aaron was doing and share in the excitement of the day. The nurses would quickly become very attached to their new charge. Within the first couple of days, Aaron had won the hearts of all those who would be caring for him in the next few weeks. They would come into his room just to talk or to see if he was comfortable. He was given the nick name, "The Hugmister," because of his generous and loving spirit of thankfulness when anyone would do anything for him, no matter how small.

It was in those first few days; Aaron was pondering a new email address. He wanted something that would tell the world how he felt and who he was. I tried to instill in all my children they must "Leave their mark" in this world, even if only on one other person's life. This new website he declared one afternoon would be named "Scars Are Not Forever," so simply stated and yet so true...

Later that afternoon Al Moore headed back home and Don Oneal and I stayed at the hospital, making sure the nurses knew how to take care of our Aaron. That evening as we left, Don to go home and I to return to my room, we stepped on the empty elevator and as the doors closed, I lost it. I started to cry and sob; Don just put his arms around me and said, "Just let it out."

I guess he had been waiting for me to reach the point of losing my emotional control, and he was ready for it. All I could manage to say in between sobs was, "I'm just so proud of him." No anguish or pity, just pride…

The following afternoon, Aaron was settling into his new room when two of the Marine Liaisons brought in a couple of lap quilts. We were told they came from all over the country and from a variety of quilting groups as well as individuals. We didn't know the history and tradition behind these beautiful quilts, but we were learning of the commitment and generosity of so many others…

As we continued to receive even more quilts, the story's behind them became a part of my daily conversations with other mothers and wives. We cherished each and every one of them as we tried to imagine the person who made them from the signature and location stitched on the back. One thing we all agreed on, comfort was found under the warmth of the love that went into the making of each one…

They came in a variety of forms and sizes, some were very intricate, others were crocheted and some just appeared neither signed nor dated. Most were lap size and some would cover a queen size bed. These quilts brought comfort, not only to the patients but their families as well. Every child of a wounded warrior as well as mothers, wives and family members could be seen with one.

In the days that followed while Aaron tried to find peace in his sleep, I would lay one of the quilts over him. The nightmares were so bad he would ask me to have the nurse's strap his arms down. Aaron would jerk so hard while he slept that he was afraid of hitting his arms and hands against the railings of his hospital bed.

When Aaron would drift off to sleep, his whole body would thrash about while dreaming. I could not imagine the horror he was re-living every time his eyes would close. But if the outward appearance was any indication, then it had to be pure Hell. I was frustrated and angry, *why couldn't I soothe my son as I did when he was a child?* I will never understand the horror of what he had seen and what he was still going through...

As the days went on without showing any sign of relief from the nightmares, Aaron mentioned them to one of his doctors. There was a medication that would not stop the nightmares, but would keep him from remembering them when he woke. This was a miracle for Aaron and with this new drug added to his arsenal, it would enable him to rest. The fear of closing his eyes would no longer disrupt his sleep. Even though Aaron did not remember the nightmares he was having, it was heart wrenching for me to watch.

Night after night I would sit by his bed and eventually lay down beside him. I would hold him while trying not to hurt his wounded body, yet still giving it all I had to keep him from jerking so hard. I was grateful that he didn't remember the battles he fought in those sleeping hours, but I can never forget them. I couldn't keep them away and holding Aaron was helping me more than him. At the very least, I hoped he felt the comfort of my arms through the darkness…

Aaron was so relieved by the freedom from not remembering the nightmares. Yet, he knew there were others on the burn ward who must be suffering from the same horrible night visions. As soon as Aaron was able to walk outside of his room, he made it a point to talk to the other wounded warriors about this medication. All, whom Aaron spoke to, were suffering the same way he had been or had just been given the drug and were as impressed with it as he was.

At one point, a young woman arrived at the hospital after being injured in Iraq. She had been a victim of an IED explosion and suffered burns on her arms and neck. She wasn't injured as badly as Aaron on the outside, but her unseen wounds were just as traumatizing. As soon as Aaron heard she was on the burn ward, we both went to her room to ask if she was having any problems sleeping. She explained her nightmares, and he knew. Aaron told her, and her mother, about the medication.

We would continue to check-in on them each day while she remained in the hospital. The young woman's mother would talk with me, out of sight from the two of them. They were both so grateful Aaron had made the effort to come down the hall that day. He had been there to help her daughter get through a horrible experience, and she thanked me for helping her to deal with everything around them.

This would be the beginning of a new purpose in my life. I knew I needed to help others who were just a few weeks or months behind where Aaron and I had been. With words of encouragement and the insight I had from my experiences, I could help them get through some of the worst times of their lives.

It is a horrible thing to watch your child suffer, and anything I could do to make one moment a little easier was what I had to do. Over the next couple of years, Aaron would call with a mother who was living the same experience which he and I had shared; who needed to talk to someone, and that someone would be me...

Those first two weeks were very difficult for Aaron while he was adjusting to a new routine of care. The physical therapy was set up to be done in his room because he was still too weak for the trip to the gym. It was important to keep this on-going routine consistent to get the best results for the recovery of his arms and hands. I would almost always leave the room. I couldn't bear to watch the pain inflected on Aaron as they pulled and massaged giving his joints and muscles a good work out. After a couple of weeks, Aaron was able to join the others in the room setup for physical therapy. He was glad to be out of his hospital room for a few hours. But the therapy was much more aggressive and painful.

Visitors to the burn ward were fairly common and would range from all ranks of military personnel to politicians as well as music and film celebrities.

Aaron, wearing the head band, in the therapy room with several visitors.

Aaron found it difficult to see everyone who wanted to come through his door. The nurses began screening these visitors, always asking him before allowing them to enter. The nurses who took care of Aaron had become very protective of their patient. He always saw any Marine who came, and he respected the visits from higher ranking officers as well.

Aaron's voice was barely a harsh whisper after the intense heat of the explosion had seared his vocal cords. The one word he would whisper to me over and over was "Kiss." I would never hesitate, knowing I almost lost the chance to ever kiss him again.

One visitor Aaron agreed to see was an Army General who had his son, who was also in uniform, and a couple of others with him. They entered the room when I had stepped out and I was unaware of their presence when I walked back in. Aaron's back was to me when I returned and I stood just inside the door, listening and not wanting to interrupt.

When he became aware of my presence, Aaron raised his arm motioning for me to come to his side. He looked up as I came close and whispered "Kiss." I leaned down and did as he asked before being introduced to the others in the room.

The General and his group quickly said their goodbyes and as he walked up to me, I noticed tears in his eyes. He hugged me with the desperation of a father, not a General, who had just seen the reality of what his own son might one day face.

Once again I realized the impact Aaron and I had on the people we came into contact with. This reinforced my desire to have a positive effect on anyone I would meet in the future. I wanted so much to help the families and friends of our wounded. I was learning more each day and there would always be others who were a few steps behind where I was, who needed a hand to hold and I had a need to be the light along their path...

One Sentence

One afternoon about five weeks into his recovery, Dr. Renz came into Aaron's room to discuss a surgery scheduled for the next day. It was to be another skin graft onto his arms and hands. This would be an inspection of sorts, to determine how well the previous grafts were coming along. He would be taking a skin graft from the top of Aaron's head. Both of his legs had not yet healed from previous grafts.

I was still staying across the street from BAMC at the Powless. When I left that night; Aaron was in good spirits and kidding around with the nurses as usual. I felt comfortable about the next morning's surgery and Aaron did not seem to be nervous. He had taken his sleeping medications and was feeling relaxed and comfortable. I quietly left his room after kissing him on the forehead.

The next morning, I walked into Aaron's room to find him still sleeping. He liked to sleep as long as he could before surgeries because he could not eat or drink anything. I sat down in the chair next to his bed and quietly watched my son. It did not matter how many times he went through those doors to surgery, each one was more difficult than the time before.

I knew the statistics; one in one-hundred just didn't wake up from being put under anesthesia. The rule was Aaron could not go through those doors until I kissed him. Everyone knew this, from the nurses to the doctors and even the cleaning staff. Especially the transport people, who took Aaron to the surgical arena, knew to stop for a moment. I would not let any of my three children, husband or any loved one of mine go into surgery without a kiss and one more "I Love You."

Aaron began to squirm in his hospital bed, but clearly did not want to wake up just yet. The nurse opened the door, peeked in, looked at me and said she would give him ten more minutes. Aaron's room was directly across from the nurses' station. When the nurse opened the door to his room all the chatter from the shift change came flooding in. Aaron began to move around in his bed arranging the various cords from the nurses call button to the IV in his foot.

The IV would be moved from vein to vein every time one would fail. This was always a very painful process for Aaron to endure. It was difficult to find a good vein after so many had failed. Just getting one IV started would usually take several sticks before one would be successful.

Aaron looked over at me in the chair and said, "Kiss." Every time I entered or exited his presence, if I had not kissed him, he would request one in this one word fashion. I was so grateful to be able to kiss him. So many mothers did not have the ability or opportunity to kiss their child who had gone to war...

The nurse reappeared and Aaron was wide awake, sitting up in his bed with a pleasant look on his face. He spoke to the nurse, who had become so close to him in the couple of weeks he had been on the burn ward, about getting this show on the road. She replied with a quick, "You are the boss," and proceeded to prep him once again for surgery.

Soon, the anesthesiologist came in to talk to Aaron about the surgery to be done that morning. He was making sure we did not have any questions or needs before he went under the anesthesia. Then in came Dr. Renz and a couple of residents who would be at his side during the surgery. After everyone completed their questions with Aaron, all the doctors went to the surgery center and began scrubbing up.

The only one left in the room was the surgical nurse who read the permission form for surgery to us. As she read, Aaron and I listened with an unconcerned attitude, because of the routine request for surgery we heard so many times before. However, this one had a phrase added to the list of surgical procedures which were to be completed that day; neither Aaron nor I had heard this possibility before. Dr. Renz had not mentioned it when he was in the room earlier.

The transport people from surgery had just arrived as the nurse informed us of the possibility of "amputation" on the list. She then asked me to sign the permission paper for Aaron. I looked at him, with hesitation, as he gave me a nod. I signed the paper and handed it back to the nurse.

Aaron knew whatever had to be done would be done. When the nurse read that word, Aaron and I looked at each other with huge eyes and a question hanging between us in the silence. As she left, the transport team loaded Aaron on to the gurney and proceeded toward those big double doors, which lead to the surgical center. As always, they stopped at the doors to allow me to kiss Aaron. His eyes were still huge, as we did not know whether he would come out of surgery without fingers or hands. There had not been time to ask any questions or discuss the possibilities between the two of us. As I bent down to give Aaron a kiss, he whispered in my ear with the desperation of a three year old asking for a chocolate bar at the checkout in Wal-Mart, "Mom Pray!" I responded with a short prayer whispered gently, but with absolute faith, into his ear. Aaron whispered back, "Thank you Mom, I love you." I responded with my love for him... Then he went through those doors, still looking back at me with those big blue eyes until they turned a corner as the doors closed.

Aaron had no idea when he went through those doors; my resolve to be strong for my baby was gone. I rushed into the restroom and started a crying, sobbing discussion with God, which lasted for some time. I'm glad no one else needed to come in there. My human weakness was getting the better of me. I had to get back in the fight and give him to God; this is the only way I would have the strength to wait the three hours I had been told Aaron would be in surgery. Only then would I know the outcome of this operation.

I continued to talk to God, as I washed my face and pulled myself together, before I went back into the waiting room. After sitting in the waiting room for a few minutes, I decided to go back to Aaron's room. There, the nurses kept checking on how the surgery was going for me. I say for me, but they were just as concerned as I was. Aaron had a way of always making you feel more important than he was. All those who had been around him from the nurses, doctors and even the housekeepers felt this and responded back with all the tender loving care they could give.

As I waited, I thought about one of the housekeepers who had been cleaning Aaron's room from the day he arrived in the Intensive Care Burn Unit, and continued when he had been moved on to the main burn ward. In the first couple of weeks, he was on a respirator and couldn't speak. But as the days turned into weeks, the housekeeper learned to sense when Aaron was having a good day or a bad one. She saw those blue eyes watching her and nicknamed him "Blue." She would speak to him as she went about her cleaning duties. "Good morning, Blue," she would say as she discerned the level of suffering in those striking, watchful eyes. She fell in love with a boy who was so badly hurt, and yet always showed her a smile through his eyes.

When he was off the respirator and the tube removed from his throat, he was able to speak. He would tell her "thank you," every time she would clean his room. Just outside his room, every day she was there, she would hug me and tell me how much she loved us, and how we were constantly in her prayers.

After about a week, will maybe it was more like three hours, a nurse came in to Aaron's room and told me he was in recovery and Dr. Renz would be in to talk to me in a few minutes. I was on the edge of my chair waiting. I could not sit still, so I started pacing up and down the hall just outside Aaron's room, watching for the doctor to appear. The nurses started to engage me in conversation as a way of distracting me. They were just as nervous as I was as they waited for Aaron to be returned to his room. Those nurses always came through, for us both...

I turned and saw Dr. Renz walking from down the hall, toward me. I was frozen as I stood there waiting for him to get to me; it seemed as if he were walking in slow motion. When Dr. Renz reached me, he asked me to step inside Aaron's room. He closed the door and began to describe how the surgery had gone. His first comments were that Aaron had come through with flying colors as usual, and I could see him in about thirty minutes or so. The nurses in the recovery room would call this room number to let me know when I could go back and see him.

Next, Dr. Renz began to show me with his hand what he had amputated from Aaron's right hand. The thumb had been removed down to his first joint and the index finger down to its second joint. When he left, I praised The Lord for not taking more of Aaron and waited for the phone to ring so I could see him.

The burns on his right hand were the most severe with third and possibly fourth degree burns. The doctors continued to put layers of grafted skin around each finger to save them. To me, this surgery showed the success of the hard work the surgeons had done...

The phone rang and I jumped as I grabbed it from its cradle. The nurse on the other end told me they were ready to bring Aaron back to his room. She asked me to please wait in the room and they would bring him out in a few minutes. Once again I was in a holding pattern. I hoped the nurse was correct in her calculation of the time it would take them to move Aaron out of recovery and back to his room. I knew when he would come the nurses on the ward would keep me at bay, so to speak, until they had him settled in the hospital bed in his room.

One of the nurses from the desk outside Aaron's room came in to let me know he was on his way. I moved out of the room and stood by the nurses' station so they could move things around for the transfer of Aaron to his bed. Just as Aaron was approaching the doorway to his room, the attendants stopped so I could kiss him. The nurses could tell he was agitated and wanted to get him settled in his room and as comfortable as he could be, in his own bed. I stood back and let them do what needed to be done. At first, I was informed Aaron's blood pressure was a little high, so they were going to be watching him closely. Now it was my turn to go in and sit with him, watching him, waiting for him to wake enough to talk about the surgery.

As soon as I entered Aaron's room, I looked at the bandages on his right hand and could see exactly how the two digits had been amputated. They were just as the doctor had explained it to me. As I was leaning over Aaron, he opened his eyes and looked up at me and asked, "What did they do?" I explained, using my hand, how they had amputated the two fingers. He listened and watched intently and then looked into my eyes and replied, "I can live with that."

So nonchalantly accepting, I knew he was dealing with a relief that only God was hearing. The nurse came in and said Aaron's blood pressure was back to normal, I turned and bit my lip as he drifted back to sleep…

Purple Heart Ceremony

Six weeks after his injury, Aaron was told there would be a Purple Heart ceremony the following day. There were several wounded heroes scheduled to receive their awards. There were so many burn victims, amputees, as well as multiple injury warriors at BMAC fighting to gain a portion of their lives back. There was so much courage in each of the patients I met, and in their families who were with them. My heart sank when another would come through those doors.

Aaron mentioned the ceremony to me, but I didn't think he would be able to attend anything outside his room. He was struggling to prepare himself for the ceremony. Aaron was still extremely weak, and the surgeries were taking a heavy toll on his ability to stand for any length of time. He also wanted to be able to salute when he was presented with his Purple Heart. Because of the scar tissue forming on the inside of his elbows, this was not a possibility. The skin grafts were still a constant cause for concern and this also encumbered his ability to straighten or bend his arms completely.

The next morning a couple of Marine Liaison's came into Aaron's room to check on how he was feeling. Aaron, being who he is, didn't want to let anyone down so he replied with some hesitation in his voice, that he was fine. As the time grew closer and when his father came into his room, Aaron told him he just couldn't do it that day. His legs were causing him so much pain, on top of what he was dealing with from the burns. Aaron's father let him know he would handle it and told Aaron the decision was his. I didn't want Aaron feeling as though he was disappointing or inconveniencing anyone. His welfare was my first concern.

There is absolutely no way anyone can imagine what a burn victim must go through!!! I never understood, and still cannot comprehend how complex and painful skin grafts are. Even while I watched my son go through this horrendous process, it was still unimaginable.

Burn victims go through a repetition of skin grafts, healing, therapy and debriding. This process is repeated over and over again for weeks, months and even years. These surgeries and procedures are very difficult for any mother to watch her child go through. Every time Aaron would go into surgery for another skin graft, I dreaded what would be coming next. I knew I would (once again) find myself falling short, in the pillar of strength department that all children expect their mothers to maintain. I expected this in myself…

When it comes to watching one of your children entering a process where they are going to be in degrees of extreme pain for several weeks at a time, only to be repeated over and over again; HOW, HOW, HOW can any mother keep up the strength to convince her child, "It will be better soon, I'm here, and you're not alone?"

It is impossible, you will fail, you will cry for help; you will be overcome with panic that only a mother who cannot make the "boo-

boo's" go away can know. Every one of us comes to the realization that we need help. We are not the perfect caregiver and our child needs much more than we can give. But, we will not relinquish "overseeing" that our child receives all the care and attention they need.

On July 10, 2005, eight weeks after Aaron had been injured, a very dear friend, Samantha Jones came into his room. We had both come to love and cherish Sam with all our hearts. She has a way of bringing joy in with her when she enters the room. She also represented **Soldier's Angels**; she truly was one to us.

Aaron and I soon learned there would be a Purple Heart Ceremony for my very special Marine in approximately two hours. Lt. Col. Brian Smallwood would be performing the ceremony in a conference room down the hall from Aaron's room. We then learned several dear friends we had made in the eight weeks since Aaron's arrival at BAMC would be there.

I was shocked we had not been advised earlier. Aaron's stepfather of 10 years, his grandparents, brother and sister were all too far away to arrive in San Antonio in time to see Aaron awarded the Purple Heart. I didn't say a word and just let the joy of the moment flow for Aaron. It would have meant so much to my father, a retired Marine and terminally ill with Pancreatic Cancer, to see his grandson receive the Purple Heart. Later, I would have a lot of hurt people to talk to.

I helped Aaron prepare what he wanted to wear and helped him dress. I didn't have time to go back over to my room and change clothes or even fix my hair. But I didn't care as long as Aaron was holding up alright.

Sam came back to Aaron's room and took some pictures for us to remember this very special moment in his young life. At 23, Aaron had already experienced more than most would in a lifetime...

Aaron and I sitting on his bed, then and always, he turned to me and said, "Kiss."

Then it was Sam's turn!!!

The three of us walked down to the conference room where the ceremony was to be held. Nurses and physical therapists were following us. People from all around the hospital who had come to know Aaron, were there to watch. Some people who had been visiting him, had been notified of the ceremony, and were there. Sam and a friend of hers asked me to sit with them, and I did. She had plenty of tissues and I needed someone with a good supply. I just kept thinking of all the mothers who didn't have the chance to see their child receive their Purple Heart...

As Lt. Col. Smallwood stepped up to the front of the small room, everyone turned their attention toward him and became very quiet. The words he spoke, with such honor about Aaron and the Purple Heart, brought tears to most eyes. Then he called for Aaron to come stand beside him as he stated the words on the official document.

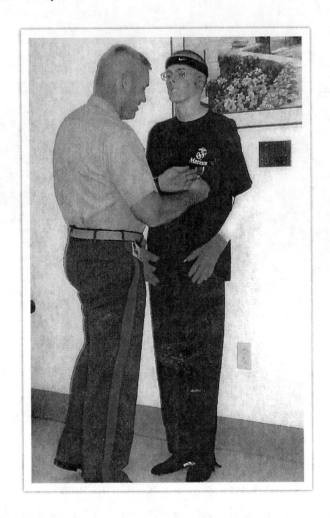

I choked back a sob as Aaron tried to raise his arm in an attempt to salute. I had tears running down my cheeks as did most in the room.

Much to my surprise, Lt. Col. Smallwood called me to the front of the room and pinned a lapel size Purple Heart on my collar. Aaron stood next to me as I sobbed through the whole thing...

As if the awards ceremony had not been enough, to top it off, Aaron was presented with his first set of Dress Blues complete with medals. At this time he was a Lance Cpl. and Aaron quickly completed the requirements to be promoted to the rank of Corporal.

General James F. Amos had been one of the first interviews Aaron had done while stationed at Camp Lejeune. He continued to keep track of Aaron after he was wounded and asked the Marine Liaison's on base, to make sure he was always available on each of his visits to BAMC.

The following week, Aaron was scheduled for another surgery. All seemed to go well, then a couple of days later he began to run a fever. The doctors and nurses watched him closely over the next two days. The fever could have come from many sources. A virus or infection or maybe pneumonia had reared its ugly head in Aaron's weakened body.

As Aaron's fever continued to climb the doctors began to rule out some of the possible causes. His lungs were clear, so the possibility of pneumonia was ruled out as the cause. But, his white blood count was very high and this meant Aaron's body was fighting something.

When I was standing at the nurse's desk, talking to Aaron's nurse, she began to share with me about a virus. This particular virus came back with almost all the patients from Iraq. It was unique to that part of the world, which made our military personnel highly susceptible because they had no immune system tolerance against it.

The longer they were deployed to the Iraqi area, the more likely it was they would come down with it. As a medical community, our doctors still new little about it or how it could be treated. This virus had only been recently identified and an antibiotic had not yet been developed. This virus could range from moderately severe too deadly. By the beginning of the third day, I was not only nervous, I was just plain scared!!!

Aaron had been in Iraq a short time, so his chances were good this might not be the cause of his fever, *but what then?* This had to be controlled quickly as Aaron's fever continued to rise and the doctors did not want to give him a generic antibiotic. They wanted to wait three more days for the cultures to identify the exact virus or infection. This would allow them to give Aaron a very specific drug to fight whatever it was.

This was not an acceptable plan when Aaron was already heading into his fourth day with no appearance of recovering. He could not lie around another three days; I was becoming very fearful as to how long this process was taking. But, no one was listening to me.

Don Oneal had been at the hospital every day since Aaron had arrived. He had been watching this drama and was as fearful for Aaron as I was. But, one thing about Don was that he never, and I mean never, let anyone see him lose his calm, always in control of himself, demeanor.

This was the situation that broke the proverbial camel's back, for Don Oneal. He had been waiting and watching over Aaron as if he were one of his own children. This course of action made no sense to him and it was time to get with the program or get out of the way! I was coming down the hall, when I spotted a very upset man, Don, surrounded by nurses while he was talking to the doctor in a rather loud tone. This got loader and loader as he continued with the conversation. Don was a tall man, but he seemed to get taller and taller as he got louder and louder. It was easy to see the Marine in him coming to the surface.

I heard the last part of this discussion as Don Oneal interjected; "This boy almost lost his life on the battlefield, and I'll be Damned if I'm going to sit by and let him die in this hospital!" The doctor turned and walked away, and the nurses who were listening went back to their stations. Within a few minutes, Aaron's nurse was hanging a bag of antibiotics on Aaron's IV pole. It was running wide open and giving Aaron the maximum amount he could receive. I believe Don Oneal saved my sons life that day...

I sat in Aaron's room watching as the bag of antibiotics emptied and another was hung on the IV pole. I couldn't keep up with how many bags he went through that night. But, around midnight Aaron began to stir. Encouraged I leaned over to look at him. Aaron opened his eyes, ever so slightly, and whispered, "Kiss."

Late the next day the doctors announced they had determined which strain they were fighting. Now the antibiotic could be switched over to a very specific one that would work even more efficiently and faster. Aaron's fever was beginning to drop by morning. I was one very grateful mother, for Don's "prayer meeting," the day before. Slowly but surely, Aaron started to come  back to his old, jovial self. I don't think he knew just how close he had come, once again, to "Heaven's Door." Aaron was always surrounded by Angels, but this time, one of them had Marine wings on...

Surgery after Surgery

While Aaron was at BAMC, he had almost forty surgeries. Most of them skin grafts. When Aaron would go through those doors for another surgery, for me it was as if he were going for the first time all over again. It never got any easier or routine to let him go, as time passed from days to weeks. Then, as it continued from months into years of surgeries, each one became more difficult than the one before. Every time he would be "put under," fear would flood my soul. Aaron always faced each surgery with an outward appearance of, "just another day, no big deal; let's just get on with it." I wondered if he had become as good at hiding his fears from me as I had from him...

We both knew what to expect, when the surgery was to graft skin from one area of his body to his arms, hands and fingers. Skin grafts are a necessary procedure, to advance the growth of healthy tissue over the exposed burn area that had no skin left to protect it from infection. It was a very difficult thing to watch your child endure. Aaron always amazed me with his tenacity in the face of so much, as well as his commitment to continue, when I was so weak.

The thought of the skin grafts literally made me sick. Aaron would go into surgery with his arms in bandages and come out with his legs, stomach or even the top of his head in bandages, as well. The grafts from his stomach were probably one of the worst places for him to deal with as they healed. Watching him try to sit up or just raise up ever so slightly, would bring such agony to his eyes. Aaron tried to hide the pain from me, but I knew the look in those eyes better than anyone in this world...

The doctors could barely give Aaron's "Donor Sites" time to heal before they would need to take more skin from them, starting the process all over again. The grafted areas seemed to be the most painful for Aaron. When the grafted skin would come from his legs, he could hardly stand.

If you can recall ever having a very bad sunburn on your legs, then lowering them to stand and how it would cause so much pain, as the blood would flow into your burns. Then trying to stand, wrenching with pain as the weight of your body was raised up on your burnt legs. Taking one slow step, grabbing onto whatever was close to steady yourself so you could take another step, trying to get to where you were going. I remember exactly the situation I just described, after a long day in the sun. It doesn't come minutely close to what Aaron was enduring...

Watching day after day as this was done to him was unbearable for me; I couldn't imagine how Aaron could face it over and over again. We had both become very good at hiding our fears from each other. My heart wept as I watched my baby being skinned alive, time and time again. That is exactly what happens when they "Harvest" skin to be grafted.

Grafting to his face would come later, when the scar tissue had contorted and twisted his mouth and nose into unbearable and life threatening ways. Before anyone talked about grafting on Aaron's face, the plan was to release scar tissue on his nose, which would allow the skin that had been drawn back and up, to reclaim its position over the exposed cartilage. As far as the mouth was concerned, the doctor's would try cutting the sides of his mouth to open it back up and not deal with the lips until later.

At one point, Aaron's mouth had drawn in and closed to the size of a nickel. The only way I could feed him was through a funnel. I could not get enough soups, protein shakes and drinks in him to prevent Aaron from continuing to lose weight. It was my responsibility to feed my child and give him enough nourishment to survive, and I was failing. We had been down this road before when he was an infant. Eventually, the doctors intervened surgically, in an effort to open his mouth so he could eat.

This picture was taken before the doctor's had opened Aaron's mouth. You can see the challenge we faced in getting any sizable amount of food in him...

A few weeks later they began to graft around this mouth, some of the grafts they were applying to his lips and face were failing. As the graft began to die, the smell of rotting flesh would begin again. After several of these failed attempts, Aaron declared one day, "I hate the constant smell of rotting flesh!" This may sound strange, but I was grateful he could smell anything at all...

Below, Aaron and Russ Meade share a lite moment together when Russ visited Aaron at BAMC during his recovery. You can see the blackened skin on Aaron's face as it dies.

Russ and Aaron served together in Iraq as well as becoming good friends. Russ would visit often and would meet Aaron throughout the years to come, at various events. As the weeks went by, I can't count how many times Aaron's face would be covered with the blackened flesh that was dying. I don't know how he endured it day in and day out.

There would be numerous surgeries in Aaron's future at BAMC to restore his lips and mouth to a point where he could eat, as well as to give Aaron lips around the opening of his mouth.

You can see the donor site where the skin was taken from Aaron's left leg and placed over the lower part of his face. This was an attempt at bringing his nose, cheeks and mouth into a more inclusive face. The first grafts that were taken from his legs and applied to his arms reached from above his knees all the way to his shorts. The right leg has healed, leaving scars of the netting and dressings left embedded in this skin, forever.

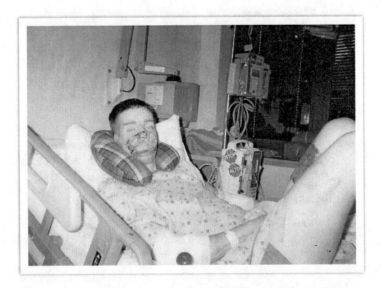

The bandages on his elbows were from an attempt to remove scar tissue, on the inside of his elbows, which had been restricting Aaron from straightening his arms. The process in which they decided to do this was one of the most horrific things I have ever seen.

They simply cut a large square chunk out of each arm and packed the open wound with gauze. Then the doctor stapled his skin to the gauze all around the edges of the wounds. This was done to keep the top layer of skin from pulling back and away from the open sites. As I stood just outside Aaron's room after having the staples removed, I heard him scream like nothing I had ever heard before as the doctor pulled the packing out of the gaping hole.

I couldn't believe what I saw...

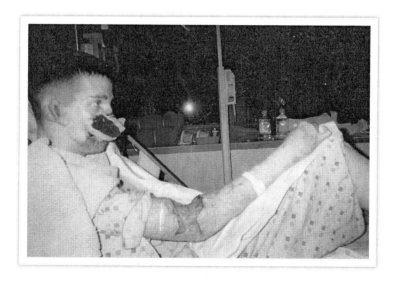

But, there sat Aaron watching the television, like it was just another day at the office.

The results from this surgery on Aaron's face were not very effective and left him with the need for more surgeries to undo what had been attempted. I couldn't understand why they continue to do surgery after surgery in an effort to restore Aaron's face, when it was obvious a Reconstruction Surgeon was what they so desperately needed. A couple of months before this surgery, the doctors tried another approach to restoring Aaron's lips. It seemed each surgery to restore Aaron's mouth was not only causing more difficulty with eating, but was causing his lips to be more and more distorted.

To form lips, the doctors decided to turn the inside of Aaron's mouth outside. This was like you pulling your lip out and down so the redness of the inside shows. This out-patient procedure was scheduled and we were told it would be a somewhat minor operation, compared to others.

When Aaron began to wake, the nurse came out to let me know I could go back and sit with him until he was ready to leave. As soon as I saw Aaron and the enormousness of this surgery, I was shocked they would even consider this an "outpatient" procedure.

The bandages used on this type of surgery, are called "Bolster's." They were stitched onto his skin to keep them in place, the main objective was to put pressure on and support the wound. The Bolsters were enormous on Aaron's upper and lower lips.

Within minutes of my entering the room, Aaron was curled up in pain trying to communicate he needed help. The nurse said she would get something more for him and within a couple of minutes he should feel some relief. She might as well have been giving him baby aspirins. After the second dose of whatever, she told me she didn't have anything else ordered to give him.

Aaron was in such agony, tears were streaming down his face, and I wasn't going to just sit back and watch my baby suffer. I told her to get orders, now! She started to argue with me and I told her to look at his stats on the monitors. Aaron's heart rate, blood pressure and everything else was elevated to a degree that made it evident he needed help now. She quickly left the room. Within a minute she reappeared and said the doctor who had performed the surgery, would be in to talk to me in just a minute.

In came a lady in scrubs, who appeared to be about seven months pregnant. She introduced herself as "The Doctor" and wanted to know what the problem was. I looked at her and just replied, "Look at him." Her response was this was just a routine out-patient procedure and he would be fine when he calmed down.

<u>This was not the thing to say to this mother!!!</u>

I got in her face and informed her there was nothing routine about what was going on with Aaron, he needed a pain medication strong enough to help him and he needed it two hours ago. She believed she could intimidate me, refusing to give him anything else and informed me Aaron could not stay in the hospital, *"Just because mommy doesn't want to take him home."*

I looked at this naive woman, and informed her this "Mommy" wasn't taking him anywhere! She WOULD admit him and to get another doctor to care for Aaron, because she was no longer on his case. "The Doctor" lowered her head and hurriedly left the room.

The nurse had been standing in the corner the whole time. She had a slight grin on her face, and said she would get the Anesthesiologist that was on duty to get orders for Aaron's pain. She also began making arrangements for Aaron to be admitted. Bless this nurse, she knew what the right thing to do was and she enjoyed watching someone tell this doctor what it was.

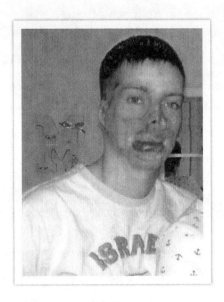

Living at the Powless

Don's Visits

I had no idea when I arrived in San Antonio that May morning, I would not go home for almost nine months, nearly as long as I was pregnant with Aaron.

Don, my husband gave me strength; he constantly and consistently was there for me. Not only was he supportive of me staying in San Antonio, he was proud of the way I was able to overcome my own health issues for my child's needs. He was probably the only person who fully comprehended the effects of Lupus on my body and emotions. Any mother, who is faced with a life changing injury of one of her children, somehow finds the strength to do whatever needs to be done.

Don and I talked on the phone every night and sometimes more than once. Those calls would last for at least an hour or more. The knowledge he was just a phone call away, at any moment, was our constant connection and made everything a bit more bearable for me...

Don and I would talk as if we were sitting across the dinner table from each other. He would tell me about his day and I would tell him about mine. During the first few weeks the calls were more frequent and focused on Aaron's progress. He loved Aaron so much and prayed for us constantly. After his first several visits, when Aaron was initially injured, Don would visit every two weeks and stay for two or three nights. In the beginning Don came as often as he could to see Aaron and to support me. He would stay with me at the Powless and got to know everyone who volunteered their time in the room down from mine, as well as other family members of wounded warriors.

There was a "Courtesy Room" down the hall from ours, on the second floor. Ms. Judith was the heart and soul of this, volunteer run, conference size room. We could always find snacks and drinks, books and movies along with a variety of gifts people made or items donated. There were computers on one end with a reading area and children's play tables, toys and games. On the other end were a couple of TV's with couches and chairs arranged around them, as well as a couple of tables with chairs. This would become a favorite gathering place for the guy's, especially during football season.

It was also where we would go to request plane fare for family members. People would donate their frequent flyer miles or money for airfare. In the time we were staying there, never was a request for airfare denied. They would also sponsor special events every week and again once a month as well as every holiday that came along. They met every need we could think of, with joyful hearts and tremendous empathy for all who lived there.

After Aaron moved in with me, when Don would come down we would get an extra room. This became quite a point of interest for the other guests as well as the staff. Everyone was aware the "visits" were our need for staying connected. Aaron could be heard making "intimate noises" from his doorway at night as we walked down the hall to our room. Everyone seemed to enjoy this, especially Aaron.

While Don was on base, as an avid exerciser, he would take daily power walks around the park. Today this is the sight of the Intrepid Center. This would serve two purposes, one was for exercise and the other, I suspect, was to let the military population know that he was my man and don't go there.

In 2005 and early 2006 the political atmosphere was tense to say the least. Everyone was very supportive of our presence in Iraq and living in a military town; patriotism was at an all-time high. On base, the alert was high and getting on base wasn't always easy. My parents drove a full size conversion van and were searched each time they came to see Aaron. Our cars were pulled over, randomly, and searched as well. We didn't mind this; in fact we appreciated the security we had. Our country did not feel safe anymore. We did not feel safe anymore. The unthinkable had landed on our doorstep as it had on many other doorsteps around our country...

Living approximately ten miles, as the bird flies, from the bombing in Oklahoma City on April 19, 1995 of The Alfred P. Murrah Federal Building, I had felt the fear of a terrorist so close. The bomb lifted the roof up from our house with a loud booming sound. I thought the heater or hot water tank had exploded in our garage causing the house to shake. I even thought maybe a plane had crashed near our home. I was afraid to venture down the hall to see what might be. Within minutes the television began to broadcast the horror of that day...

The Bombing of the Alfred P. Murrah Federal Building in Oklahoma City would remain the most destructive act of terrorism on American soil until the September 11, 2001 attacks. The Oklahoma blast claimed 168 lives, including 19 children under the age of 6, and injured more than 680 people. This blast destroyed or damaged 324 buildings within a sixteen-block radius and shattered glass in another 258 buildings.

So many of our citizens had been affected by the blast, which were not included in these numbers. Children and adults sustained emotional injuries which will never go away.

Then came September 11th of 2001 and the massive terror and loss of life that was brought that day. This quickly turned into rage at the cowardly and vicious attack on our country. This horror could not be counted by lost or changed lives. So many of our sons and daughters had their first taste of what pure evil this world holds, and they began to go to defend us from it…

When Don would take his walks, he often met other wounded warriors along the path. He was so angry at the devastating injuries of our warriors, and their suffering; it was hard for him to hold it inside. On one occasion, Don encountered a group of young men, who had suffered injuries to their arms and legs leading to amputations. He stopped and listened for a moment, then joined in the conversation by stating; "If I could just get that …. who pushed the button, in a room for five minutes…. They all joined in with, "We would too!" The conversation continued in the manner that men do when fiercely wanting to protect their own.

The faces of war were all around us, and even though there was anger inside of both Don and me, we were constantly amazed at the courage and fortitude these very young men and women showed. The carnage we saw on that base in 2005 and 2006 was only outweighed by the strength of character each one possessed...

Hold Me

Aaron and I had been living in the Powless for a couple of weeks and were getting into a routine of twice a day therapies. It was like taking your child to school, picking him up for lunch and taking him back. Then picking him up after to go home and do dinner. As you can see, Aaron was still wearing glasses which irritated his nose and what remained of his ears.

He had requested Lasik eye surgery and had seen a doctor in the offices at BAMC, but it just wasn't the right time. Aaron's mouth was slowly becoming smaller and restricted by the scar tissue. He could not even close his mouth completely. When the cold days came, he was miserable with his teeth exposed to the cold air.

At first I tried to go with him to the therapy sessions, but watching them inflect pain on him over and over again was impossible for me to watch. Day after day the therapist would massage and bend joints and muscles that had been damaged by the fire. Physical Therapy is torture with consent...

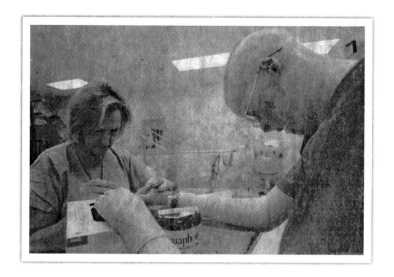

When Aaron would have appointments, I would stay with him to get the latest update on how his therapy was coming along. Sometimes, it was news of another surgery. I felt guilty about not staying with Aaron during all of his therapy sessions, but I just couldn't stand it. I tried, God knows I tried...

During the week, the therapists would teach me how to unwrap and wrap his bandages, so I could do it on the weekends. I had trembling hands, not only from being afraid of hurting him but also because of my Lupus. The therapists were always available during the weekends at the hospital to help us if I needed it.

After another difficult day for Aaron during his rehab session we returned to our room, and started talking about what to have for dinner. When he said to me, "Mom, lie down next to me and just hold me for a while." I kicked off my shoes and crawled up on the bed and scooped up his head in my arms, ever so carefully. I was so afraid of hurting him, but I needed to hold him as much, if not more, than he needed me to.

His head was snuggled up under my chin and on the hollow below my shoulder. It reminded me of when he was a tired little boy, needing the comfort of his mother's arms. As we lay there propped up on several pillows, I just stroked his hair and kissed his forehead. I was so grateful Aaron had not been burned on his forehead or eyes. When Aaron would hold a cup up to his mouth, you only saw his blue eyes and would not realize the extent of the wounds on the rest of his face.

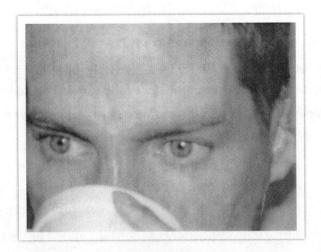

I had seen several other warriors at BAMC that looked as if they had been scalded from the top of their heads down the length of their bodies. It felt so good to just hold him in my arms...

As we were holding on to each other, Aaron turned his face up to look me in the eyes. He had a searching as well as a pleading look in those clear blue eyes of his. It was a look every mother has seen many times. But the intensity of the plea was overwhelming...

Every time one of my children would have a "boo-boo," they always came running to mommy. All it took to comfort them and make it all better was a kiss on the sight of the "hurt" and a hug with some loving and they would be on their way.

My babies eyes were saying, "Momma, Please make it go away, make me better." Oh, how I wanted to wake him from this nightmare to a beautiful, peaceful morning. As he looked from one of my eyes to the other, searching, I wanted so much to take this horrible burden from him. But how, there wasn't anything I could do, but hold him, and we both knew it...

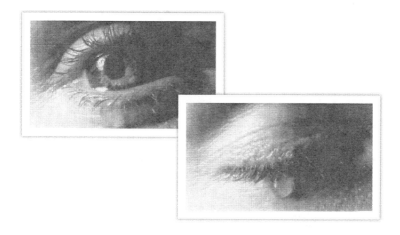

I pulled him even closer and stroked his hair a little faster while kissing his head, hoping my arms could somehow help, just a little. Oh Lord, please let it...

After about an hour, we were both getting hungry and he sat up with the question of what are we going to eat tonight? The desperation had been pushed back down where we didn't have to deal with it, for now.

Aaron decided on Pizza, that night, so I called in the order to be delivered. When the pizza came I cut it up after having used the anti-bacterial soap to sanitize my hands. Aaron was doing pretty well at feeding himself, so I was fixing my plate while he started eating. With my plate in hand, I turned around to sit next to him while we ate. I asked how his pizza was. At this time, his taste buds were still a bit scorched, and he was just beginning to get his sense of taste back. Aaron looked up at me to answer my question and started laughing. "It's great, if you like the taste of soap." he replied. I laughed and took a bite; it was horrible! But at least he could taste the soap...

I Was Blind and Now I See

One day after Aaron had finished with his re-hab for the day, we decided to roam around the lower floor of BAMC and check out a book drive that was going on. As we got closer to the Ophthalmology clinic, Aaron spotted one of the young ladies who worked for one of the doctors. She pulled Aaron in and said, "Just wait here." After a couple of minutes, the doctor came out and asked Aaron if he was ready to have Lasik's done on his eyes. Will that had been the plan all along, we were just waiting until they could get to him.

I didn't realize how bad Aaron's vision was until one day after he had been moved onto the main burn ward. I had gone in to talk with him before we thought to have him examined for glasses. I had so many other things on my mind that he was going through, I just hadn't thought about this. I asked him if he could see me as I stood over him. Aaron shook his head from side to side. So I leaned in a little closer and asked again if he could see me, again he shook his head. On the third try, I leaned in about six inches from his face and asked the question. This time he replied in a harsh whisper, "Now, I can see your face."

The doctor led us back through a maze of offices and corridors until we reached the surgery room. Aaron was taken inside and I was told

I could watch, if I wanted to, from the large window in the hall way.

The first thing that was done was to make sure Aaron was a candidate for this surgery.

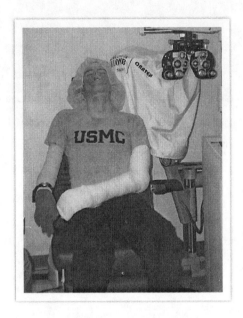

They put drops in his eyes first, and he just lay back with his eyes closed and waited for the doctor. When the doctor returned, only moments later, he began telling us everything he was going to do in the course of the surgery. He seemed as excited as we were for Aaron to have his sight improved.

They put some drops in Aaron's eyes and he relaxed for a few minutes before the surgery began. The doctor stepped out of the room while the drops took effect. About five minutes later, he returned and leaned over Aaron to check the drops effectiveness. Within minutes, the doctor was finished, and Aaron just sat there with his eyes closed until he was told he could open them. I thought he might be a little afraid to open them in case the surgery had not worked.

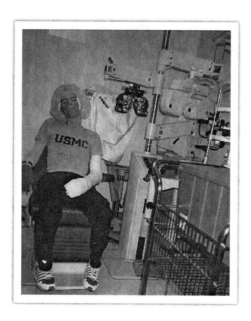

Then Aaron slowly opened his eyes and he could see!!! Aaron had worn glasses or contacts for most of his life. The doctor told him, his vision would improve over the next few hours and days.

This was a tremendous miracle for Aaron, and he couldn't what to share the experience with others. It could help so many who had worn contacts and glasses before they had been injured.

Just one more "God-Incidence" to add to our list of miracles...

All I Want

Aaron and I had been living at the Powless for a couple of months, and the weekend was coming up. It had been a hard week for him in Physical Therapy. They tried for the second time to put a cast on his right hand and wrist. This was an attempt to straighten his pinky that was frozen in a bent position and bend his wrist which had begun to freeze in a straight position.

The therapist would work on the joints for hours in order to get them loosened up, if even to a small degree. Then they would put a cast on the joint in the flexed position which it had been manipulated into. As the twisted joints would begin to try and return to their pre-manipulated position, the cast would become an aggressive weapon restricting any movement. This was a very painful ordeal for Aaron as the pressure inside the cast would grow and grow.

Most of these attempts failed when the pressure would become too painful, and Aaron couldn't stand it any longer. Within a few hours, Aaron would be struggling to deal with the pain, and by the night it was impossible to manage. We would be back at the hospital to have the cast removed. This pattern would be repeated over and over.

After the relief of having the latest cast removed, Aaron and I were discussing things to do on the weekend. We could checkout movies and go out to eat, whatever Aaron felt like doing. Then the phone rang, it was his girlfriend from Iraq, so I left the room to give them some privacy.

When I returned to the room, Aaron was still on the phone but was about to hang up. He just lay there on the bed, with his eyes closed as he prayed, holding the phone tightly. Not realizing Aaron was praying, I began to speak, but he didn't respond so I became quite. After a moment, he looked over and told me he had been praying and that's why he didn't answer. I said I was sorry for interrupting and asked how he was.

As Aaron began to tell me about the conversation, he became very emotional. He was so afraid of the future and the effect of his disfigurement on his relationship with his girlfriend, Diana, or any woman. Aaron began to pace around the room crying and ranting with anger inside of him that had been held in too long.

While this was going on I felt helpless. I had no words to comfort him and when I tried to hold him, he just couldn't be held. I was crying in anguish right along with him. When he was on the other side of the room from me, he bent over as if in pain or just exhausted, yet still sobbing and full of anger. Aaron was staring at the floor, bent over, when he turned and looked at me and said, "All I want is for someone to love me the way that you love, is that too much to expect."

I was stunned, yet the compliment Aaron had just given me was enormous. I tried to reassure him there was someone in this world who would see him and all he is along with the scars, and would love him for that special person he is on the inside. I went on to tell him how when people first see him they are taken back by the scars, but that shining spirit of his will always come through and the scars are no longer visible.

Aaron was calming down as the emotional situation was winding down inside of him. I don't know if he heard a word I said, but at least for now I could hold my son in my arms and try to will his pain away.

I few minutes later he asked for the keys to my car. I could see Aaron still had a lot of anger going on inside. He was desperately trying to find a way of coping with the reality of life with his scarred face. I gave him the keys and out the door he went. This was the first time Aaron had driven. I was hoping the freedom of taking the car would bring him a feeling of normalcy.

Aaron had been gone almost two hours and I was beginning to get worried. Then the door opened, and as he entered Aaron tossed the keys to me and quietly went into the bathroom. When he came back in the room the tight set of his jaw told me he was still struggling. I casually asked where he had been and he started talking about his trip to the Mall. Aaron had driven to the Mall without any difficulty and just walked around. He was observing the reactions of other people when they noticed his disfigured face. This little taste of freedom had been a difficult one for him.

This was a very hard, but necessary breakthrough for Aaron in coming to terms with the reality of what he would look like for the rest of his life. All the surgeries to improve his facial features had only resulted in more distortions rather than improvement.

My heart was breaking while I listened to Aaron and saw the disturbed look in his eyes. I kept trying to come up with some words to comfort him but my mind was just so full of rage at this whole way of life that had become Aaron's future. I felt helpless and discouraged, and then he changed the subject of our conversation back to his call from Diana.

Aaron told me she had a leave coming up, after six months in Iraq, and planned on visiting us after she spent a few days with her mother in Virginia. This bit of news held several questions only time would be able to answer. Even though Aaron didn't say anything, it was obvious he was torn inside. He wasn't sure how she would react to the person she would see. He was hoping Diana would realize the person she had fallen in love with was still there, behind the scarred face.

As he continued to talk about their conversation, I noticed Aaron's mood begin to change. He was becoming more confident in the feelings they had shared and the conversations they were having didn't reflect any change of heart. Now, he needed her to see what he looked like and accept the changes on the outside.

Plans needed to be made as the time grew closer for Diana's arrival. She and her mother would be flying to San Antonio and planned on staying for several days. Aaron paid for their airfare and the room they would be staying in at the Powless. I asked him if I could provide another room, one where he and Diana could have some privacy away from their mother's. He thanked me for thinking of it and gave me the go ahead to reserve a third room.

I was excited at the thought of meeting Diana and her mother. Aaron had told me how they met and when he had first seen Diana when she arrived at Camp Lejeune. When she got off the bus, he thought to himself how much she looked like me. Then when he found out her name was the same as mine, it really freaked him out.

It didn't take long for the two of them to grow close and Aaron wanted me to meet her, over the phone. Aaron told me how much he cared for Diana and soon we would talk on the phone, so I got to know her a little from those conversations. After Aaron was injured I kept in constant communication with her through emails. I wanted to make sure she had all the information about Aaron's recovery. I felt she should know everything about Aaron's injuries.

The night before one of Don's visits, I asked Aaron if he wanted him to bring my grandmothers diamond ring. It would be in our safe, and he could use it or not, whatever, it would be there. Aaron thought for a few seconds and asked to have the ring available.

When the day came, Aaron and I went to the airport to meet Diana and her mother. Aaron pointed out the escalators they would be coming down and asked me to stay back until he had greeted Diana. He was nervous and fearful, to say the least. We waited and watched for them to appear at the top and begin their descent down.

As soon as Diana and her mom appeared, Aaron pointed them out and hurried over to the bottom and waited as they slowly came down. When Diana stepped off the escalator, Aaron swept her up in his arms. Her mother stepped aside to give the two a moment alone. As we watched our children, Aaron dropped to his knee, with the ring box in hand. All I could see was Diana shaking her head up and down as Aaron rose to his feet and once again held her in his arms. Tears were running down my face as were her mother's as we both rushed to hug the engaged couple.

The next three days would be spent in a whirlwind of sightseeing and wedding plans. The hardest part was knowing Diana had to return to Iraq for another six months. But, the happiness and relief that came from this visit would be a driving force for Aaron in recovering from all his injuries, inside as well as out. After they left, it was back to the routine of more surgeries followed by continuous physical therapy.

Why Aaron

After several months of surgeries and physical therapy, Aaron and I were walking down the hall at BAMC, where he had seen a doctor or two. He seemed to be thinking about something, but he just couldn't find the right words. There was a question he wanted to ask, but was still mulling it over in his mind.

It was as though Aaron was trying to come to terms with everything that was going on around him, the explosion, his injuries and everything that happened to get him to San Antonio so fast. Why did he survive? All the people involved with his recovery, the nurses, therapist and all those people who were praying for him and sending concerned emails. People, whom he had never met, wanted to see him and interview him. Why was he being recognized?

I decided to wait for the question and not interrupt what was going through Aaron's thoughts. I could no more imagine what he was going through, emotionally, than he could know what I was.

In November of 2005, Oliver North had come to San Antonio for a book signing at a doctor's convention. He invited Aaron and me to attend his speaking engagement before the signing. Oliver first met Aaron in Iraq. His film crew had been traveling in the convoy Aaron had been assigned to accompany as the Marine combat correspondent escort. This mission was called, "Operation Matador."

Aaron and I were still living on base when the car arrived to take us downtown and to see Oliver North, and hear him speak. His assistant met us at the back door and took us to our seats on the front row. When Oliver began to talk, Aaron started slumping down in his chair. He was speaking about a young, courageous Marine, whom he met in Iraq, and how he told him to "Be careful" as they headed out on their mission that day. Aaron was that young Marine, who with his usual humor replied, "No, you be careful, I may have a camera in one hand, but I have a rifle in the other." Operation Matador and Aaron would become focal points in Oliver's speeches, television show (War Stories with Fox News), and his book titled American Heroes.

After the speeches, the doctors went to the various vendor booths that were setup in the back of the auditorium. Oliver had a booth for his book signing and his assistant took Aaron and me behind his booth. There we met, and Oliver had a little time to talk with his friend. That was when we learned there was a video of the AAV Aaron was in exploding, as well as him being loaded onto the helicopter. His assistant asked if we wanted a copy of it, and I replied, "Yes." It would take me almost two years before I could watch it...

Aaron was being recognized more and more as the months turned into years. He was asked to speak at local events, as well as some national television and radio shows. Especially around the holidays such as Veteran's Day, Memorial Day and the Marine Birthday, there would be invitations to speak and interview requests. The whole time Aaron was at BAMC there was a barrage of recognized "Stars" of television, news, sports and music that would come through to create a diversion from the everyday medical routine, as well as to show their respect to the men and women who were Heroes to them.

One of those interviews would affect Aaron's life and change the history of how VA hospitals and the private hospitals worked together. Not only Aaron's life would be forever changed, but the community of wounded and disfigured warriors would be given the gift of a much greater quality of life…

Finally the question Aaron needed to ask came stumbling, awkwardly from his lips. "Mom, when I was little, ah. Growing up, did you ever think, will, that I would be kind a…well-known or maybe kind a famous or that my life would be so different?"

At first I didn't know how to respond. I told Aaron he had always been special and even as a baby people were drawn to him. Later I thought more about his question and this is what I told Aaron:

Your life has always been different. When I carried you within me, I was different. The things of this world made me ill. Even the pollution in the air was so much more intense. It was as all I could do to take care of our family. It was a struggle to cook and watch over Sarah and Jason. Your father was out of town a lot, which made it easier in a way.

When I was in my 25th week of pregnancy, I just couldn't continue to work. My doctor agreed and I went on a medical leave. Looking back, I know now the attack that was being wagged inside of me was one to destroy you. I truly believed I would not be able to carry you to term. I even felt if you were born, you may not survive. Little did I know I would spend every day, from your birth throughout your life, fighting that which is trying to harm you?

On the Saturday night you were born, I was filled with an uncertainty I can't put into words. Something was wrong, but I didn't understand what was happening inside my body. I tried to tell your father I didn't feel right, but I wasn't in labor. I couldn't express exactly how I felt, so we decided to go to the hospital just to see what was going on and to be sure everything was alright.

It was around 12:45 on the morning of the tenth before I was in my room, awake and in control of the pain from the C-Section, when the nurse called over the intercom to see if I wanted to nurse you. I called out to her, please bring me my baby I haven't even seen him yet. The nurse who brought you to me was an angel. She calmed me and helped me hold you in the most loving way that soothed us both.

I felt the presence of The Lord in my room. That was when I first felt you were different, special. The plan for your life is one that will take the strength of Samson, the faith of Job and the love of David all wrapped up in the blood of Jesus.

I truly believe GOD created you with a very special purpose to help other's find their way through what seems like impossible life experiences. From the time you were born, until the day you go to be with The Lord you will be in a battle. *You don't have a choice, you have been chosen.*

GOD loves you as he loved David…

GOD has allowed people to see your faith through tribulation, as with Job...

GOD has given you the strength to endure...

GOD holds you close, even when you turn away...

Aaron is holding his two little ones. Behind them is the picture Tony Benson drew for him after he was injured and the two flags are from his grandfathers. My father was a Marine and his paternal grandfather was a Seabee with the Navy Construction Battalion during WWII.

I Became a Liability

In the middle of December of 2005, Aaron was making very good progress in his physical and occupational therapy. He was waiting anxiously for the return of his wife-to-be from Iraq, and continued making plans to meet Diana when she arrived on the east coast. Aaron's spirits were high, which is crucial in the recovery process for anyone healing from a traumatic injury.

I on the other hand, was struggling with one Lupus flair after another. Most of which I could hide from Aaron; he had no idea what was going on in my body until I began falling.

My legs would just disappear from underneath me, and down I would go. Most of the time this would happen when I wasn't with Aaron, which made it easier to hide. I would have skinned knees, scrapped palms and sometimes a bruise or scratch on one side or the other of my face. I could hide all this with clothes and makeup.

I thought after Christmas, when Aaron went to his fathers for a visit and I returned home for the holiday, I would get some rest and this Lupus flair would be over. Then when Aaron and I returned to BAMC after the first of the year, I would be renewed and able to continue taking care of Aaron until he married in late January or early February. The timing would all work out, nobody would know about the falling, and nobody would have to worry about me or my ability to continue to care for Aaron.

Aaron left for Rogers, Arkansas with his father and I got in my car and headed up I-35 for home. It was a 7½ hour drive and one I had made before. No changing to different highways, just straight home. I would stop on the outskirts of Fort Worth, to get something to eat and off I would go again. It would be so good to be home, I had not been there since I left on May 13th of 2005. Don brought a list of things for me each time he would come down. So gradually I had all my clothes and things with me, in the little room Aaron and I shared at the Powless.

The holidays passed and it was time to go back to San Antonio to meet Aaron and resume our existence at BAMC. On the way to San Antonio, I stopped at my usual place for a bit to eat and some gas. As I was walking out and down the sidewalk to my car, I fell. No reason, I just didn't have any legs to support me. I went down hard on my knees, and with my hands I barely caught my head from hitting the concrete. I was stunned for a few seconds, and just stayed down until I could evaluate my condition. Before I could move, two gentlemen were kneeling by my side; they had seen me go down from the window inside the store.

They asked if I was alright and I assured them I was, so they helped me to my feet and stood with me for a minute to make sure I was alright. I thanked them and turned, walked to my car and got in. I sat there a few minutes and felt alright. My knees were scrapped and my hands stung, but I could still drive the three and half hours to San Antonio.

When I got back at the Powless, Aaron had not yet arrived. He was just a few minutes behind me, and it was good to see him and listen to him talk about his trip and seeing all his friends. I didn't mention my fall and kept my injured knees and hands out of sight.

The next few mornings were uneventful, as we got back into the routine of physical therapy and doctor appointments. All the nurses and therapists were happy to see Aaron back, and everyone had stories to tell about their own holidays.

About two weeks after returning, Aaron and I were just hanging out on a Saturday morning. I was still in bed while he was in the chair between our beds, watching something on the television. I decided to get up, and as I started to stand, once again, I had no legs to support me. Aaron's chair was pushed close to the television, so I fell behind him. My head hit the railing of his bed with a loud crash. Aaron jumped up and came to my side. He was hysterical, asking if I was alright. I kept telling him I was, I just need to lay there a minute before I tried to stand again.

Aaron was so upset, he just kept asking if I was sure I was alright and I kept reassuring him I was fine. Then he said the one thing I will never forget. With tears in his eyes, he said, "Mom I've never been so scared, not even when I was on fire!" That is when I knew, I had become a liability to Aaron's recovery.

I spoke to the Marine in charge at BAMC and told her what happened and how I felt I couldn't stay any longer, or Aaron would be taking care of me instead of the other way around. She assured me Aaron was strong enough to be assigned to a barrack on base, close to the hospital, and the others would assist with the move into the barracks and get him settled. "That is what occupational therapy is all about," she said. I also spoke to one of the physical therapist. I wanted to make sure they knew I would be leaving as soon as Aaron was assigned to a barrack, so they would be aware of the help he would need to move.

One morning, Aaron came rushing in after a meeting and told me he had been assigned to a barrack. I had already been packing while he was gone and carrying my things down to the car. Aaron looked around and said, "Are you leaving already?" I told him yes, everything would be taken care of to move him and I needed to get back home.

I'll never forget the way he sat on the floor, across from the door, just watching as I pushed the last piece of luggage out the door. I was leaving my child to the care of others. Aaron felt it and I felt it. When the door closed, I started crying and I'm sure he did as well. We were both lost. I felt so guilty for not being stronger; mothers aren't allowed to be sick…

It took me two days to get home. I was so sick, exhausted and upset I kept running off the side of the road. By the time I reached Fort Worth, I knew I wasn't going to make it any further without killing myself and possibly someone else. I pulled over, got a motel room and spent the night. I checked out around noon after a very long restless night. The rest of the drive was a little over three hours and again, by the time I reached home I was struggling…

After all the preparations I made for Aaron to be moved into the barracks, not one soul came to help. So Aaron remained in the room at the Powless for several weeks. Nobody seemed to notice he was alone.

I would call to check on him, but he would not answer. I left messages; he would not return my calls. I sent emails, he would not respond. I knew he was angry with me, I was angry with me...

After not hearing from him for several days, I sent a message to his father to see if he had heard from Aaron. He always replied he had, and Aaron was fine. A couple of weeks later, I found out he had not been moved into the barracks as were the plans when I left. He finally talked to me and told me, "It's just not the way things are done in the Marines." I didn't tell him about the arrangements I made before I left. I told him, I thought the Occupational Therapy Department would see that he had the things he needed to move. And, the Marines on base would help him settle in. But, that didn't happen.

Aaron's father went down to San Antonio when he found out Aaron had not moved into the barracks. He set-up the room and moved him out of the Powless, making sure he had what he needed from Occupational Therapy to make it easier to access his new room.

I left my son in the care of others, and I failed him. It was my responsibility to make sure the arrangements were carried out as promised. Nobody else's, just mine. It would take time for Aaron to forgive me. I don't know that I will ever forgive myself. He gradually began returning my phone calls and messages over the next couple of months.

GUILT, GUILT, GUILT, GUILT, GUILT, GUILT, GUILT!!!

Before Aaron married, my father was showing the effects of the Pancreatic Cancer he had been fighting for over a year. He and I began to speak more and more as Dad's health was failing. Aaron was preparing to meet his fiancée' as soon as she arrived back in the States from Iraq. He returned from Virginia a married man and soon his wife would be assigned to BAMC, joining him in a small house on base.

Soon after my father passed on, and all my mother wanted was for Aaron to present her with his flag during the funeral ceremony. It was a last minute request and he couldn't refuse. Aaron instructed the men at the funeral home on how to fold and present the flag to him. Aaron's hands were still so tender and not very useful, so the men had to lay the flag across one wrist as he put the other hand on top to hold it. Aaron did a magnificent job of marching, turning and presenting his Grandmother with his Grandfather's flag...

My father, a retired Marine from WWII, was a gentle man with a quite spirit and a deep love and commitment for family. Kenneth Gene Lindsey survived for fourteen months after his diagnoses. He worried so much about his family, especially Aaron and how he would cope with his life. He refused to give up even when told there was no hope. Strength of character runs deep in the men of my family...

While Daddy lay in bed, he always had a quilt Aaron had sent to him by his side. I took this quilt, which was made with caring hands and given with hope to comfort, to the funeral director to be placed with my Daddy when he was cremated. My mother would tell me later, how so many people came up to her after the funeral and commented on Cpl. Aaron Mankin's presentation of the flag. She was very proud of the man her grandson had become...

By this time, Aaron had been married a couple of months. Maybe a month after the funeral, he couldn't wait to tell me they were expecting a little girl in January of 2007. Becoming a father was the most exciting thing in the world for him. Aaron so enjoyed playing the part of "Daddy" and had one question for me, "Why didn't you tell me how much fun this would be?" Oh, what joy filled me while I watched as he saw the world all new again through his child's eyes!!!

Aaron's world had taken on a whole new meaning with the birth of his daughter. The purpose of his life had become so much larger.

Several months after the birth of Madeline Paige, he was approached about having reconstructive surgery on his face in Los Angeles. Aaron was concerned about his looks becoming a source of ridicule for his daughter as she grew and made friends. He was fearful of the teasing she might have to deal with and would do anything to prevent this from happening. No matter what it took on his part, he was willing and eager.

One Man and One Marine

One evening in August of 2007, Aaron called to tell me about a man in Los Angeles. He wanted to help him with the reconstruction of his face. Aaron had spoken about this before, but was cautious about getting his hopes up. So many times he had been told a surgery was going to accomplish this or that and had been extremely disappointed, or the plan would never develop. Aaron learned to not count on anything until it happened.

This time, Aaron's voice was full of an anticipation and excitement I had not heard in a long time. He started to tell me about this man, who was on the Board of Directors at the UCLA Medical Center. He knew this man was very influential, not only with the Medical Center but he was also a good friend of General James F. Amos. So there was a military connection and a private sector connection as well.

Aaron asked if I would go to California with him and see everything that was being talked about, as well as go with him to several appointments for his first surgery. The surgery had been scheduled for the day after Aaron's appointments. This would be a 10 day trip. The enthusiasm coming from him was a joy to hear, and the things he began to share with me sounded as though he had finally been presented with a plan which had all the possibilities of changing his life.

Aaron and I boarded a plane and started a new chapter of recovery, one which would be filled with miracles in both of our lives. So many people would be affected by the potential of this opportunity that was so graciously given to Aaron; it would change the course of history for us all. This "Gift" would not only change Aaron's life, but so many others as well.

It all started with "One Man and One Marine."

When Aaron and I stepped off the plane we were met by the man from UCLA who would be heading up this new venture. Shannon O'Kelley was the Administrator of this new program and responsible for the development of its purpose. He was also the Associate Director of Operations-Clinical Services for UCLA Hospital Systems. Shannon would personally meet us at the airport and escort us to the UCLA Tiverton House, where we would be staying while Aaron recuperated from his surgery.

Shannon would become a special friend to both Aaron and me. He cared so much about this program and wanted to make sure everything ran smoothly for all involved. He would walk us to Aaron's appointments, and make sure we were comfortable with everything we would be experiencing in the week to come. Watching Aaron and Shannon as their bond grew, was like watching two kids in a candy store as they talked about new phone technology or a new movie that was out and the hope for the future.

As we walked down the sidewalks, between the medical center and The Tiverton House, Aaron and Shannon would discuss not only the boyish side of life, but they would banter around the challenge of giving a name to this program. Eventually, all those involved would settle on the name, "Operation Mend."

Aaron Mankin and Shannon O'Kelly

The personal relationship which was formed between these two would last a lifetime. No matter what, Aaron new Shannon was always as close as a phone call away.

When we arrived at The Tiverton House for the first time, we were greeted and treated like royalty. From the managers to the housekeepers, they all were so excited about us being there. They had all been "infected" with the desire to help this wounded warrior who was so badly disfigured.

When Aaron and I entered our suite, we were pleasantly surprised at the baskets of fruit and other goodies that had been placed in our rooms. We had adjoining rooms so we could easily move about. Aaron would sneak the recliner from my room, as if I wouldn't notice, into his. He was more comfortable sitting in this reclining chair, especially after one of his surgeries.

During the next couple of days, before Aaron was scheduled for surgery, I met everyone in the "group" of people who would be caring for him. Dr. Timothy Miller was the one who would be doing all the surgeries on Aaron's face, as well as coordinating visits with other departments to help with his various needs. I was welcomed with hugs as everyone became to know me as, "Mom."

Dr. Miller was the Chief of Plastic and Reconstructive Surgery at the UCLA Medical Center. He was the former Chief of Plastic Surgery at the West Los Angeles (Wadsworth) V.A. and an Army Captain during the Vietnam War. He understood what it was like to come back from war and try to find meaning in life. The unseen injuries of war had affected him as well.

When he returned from the Vietnam War, if it had not been for his entry into a Residency program, he felt he would never have left his apartment. This insight would be crucial in dealing with Aaron's PTSD in the future as their relationship and understanding of each other grew.

Patti Taylor would be the nurse-case manager, who would make sure we were where we needed to be, when we needed to be everywhere. When Patti learned of Aaron, who had been badly disfigured in Iraq, would be coming to UCLA Medical Center for Facial reconstruction, the retired Army nurse insisted on volunteering. She would not only be Aaron's case manager but a guiding light for me as well.

Patti not only navigated us through the appointments and surgeries, she made sure we were taken care of. I can't tell you how many times she made me go eat or rest. Patti would get in my face and tell me, "Never, ever walk from the Medical Building back to your room after dark!"

Patti had the schedule and made sure Aaron was always at the front of the line when it came to lab work, prescriptions and other appointments. She was a gem and her soft heart would be a driving force in keeping Aaron on course. Patti had fought for the opportunity to be a part of this new program and we were not only fortunate but grateful to have her by our sides.

After the appointments were finished and Aaron and I were back at the Tiverton House, a phone rang. It was Dana Katz on Aaron's cell phone, they talked for a few minutes then he told me what the agenda was for the evening. Dana's husband, Todd, would be picking us up and taking us back to their home for dinner.

Aaron told me Todd and Dana were the son and daughter-in-law of Ron and Maddie Katz, and they would be checking in on us making sure we had everything we needed. We were to feel free to call and ask any question or request anything from them; they were our family guardians while we were away from home. Their home became our home.

I was impatiently waiting to meet them, Aaron had told me so much and yet so little about the Katz connection. That night, I would learn how all this had come to be.

When Todd arrived to pick up Aaron and me, he explained he needed to stop by his dads for a minute before going on to his home. When we pulled inside the gate and went up the steps, Todd opened the door and we followed him through the house to his father's office. Ron Katz looked up and saw he had been invaded, with a smile on his face he reached a hand out to Aaron, while telling Todd where to get whatever he had stopped in for. Aaron introduced me and followed Todd out of the office. Ron asked me to sit down and he started to tell me about how this whole thing had started.

Ron began by telling me it was right here, in his office, on that television set, he saw Aaron for the first time. He was watching the Lou Dobbs Show; as he interviewed a young Marine at Brooke Army Medical Center, who was horribly scarred. Yet, the captivating personality came shining through, as this young man answered the questions about what was next for him in his recovery. Aaron rather flippantly had remarked the next thing to be done was to fix the beautiful part, to make him good looking again.

Ron told me as he watched Aaron and looked at his scarred and disfigured face, he thought to himself, "That boy is not going through life with that face." He then went upstairs and asked his wife, Maddie, to come down and look at something on the television. Ron re-played the program, and as Maddie watched and Ron talked, she looked at him and said, "Oh yes, we must do something."

I was speechless, and unable to find the words to express my emotions for what I had just been told. I was so grateful for everything. There's not a deep enough place inside me to express the gratitude for what was being done for my child.

Maddie and Ron Katz

The thought of this man, watching one Marine, at exactly the right time and being inspired to insure a better life for my son, was and is, beyond words... (G.I.)

Todd and Aaron re-appeared, as I was fighting back tears, through the office door and we left with the assurance Ron and Maddie would be over shortly to join us for dinner. As soon as I enter the front door of Todd and Dana's house, I felt the open hearts of their family and was instantly made to feel at home. We would spend many nights like this one, at our home away from home.

Operation Mend Begins

After Monday's appointments, Tuesday morning Patti picked us up and escorted us up to the Outpatient Surgery Center. This would become the routine for the next several years as Aaron continued to have surgery after surgery.

Patti would get the nurses in the loop, and we would start the pre-op check list of things to be signed, clothes to be changed, IV's to start and consults with the doctors involved.

When Dr. Miller arrived, to everyone's surprise, this very serious man was sporting his camouflage hat.

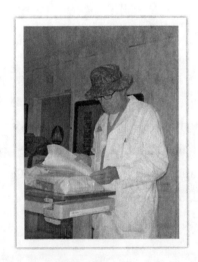

This lightened the mood considerably, and after a few military jokes exchanged between the two, it was back to the business of what was going to be done during this first surgery.

Dr. Miller would take out a purple marker and draw on Aaron's face the places he would be working.

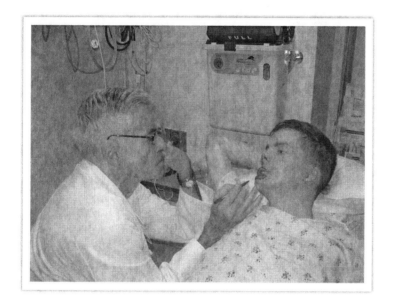

There would be several surgeries to come, in preparation for the more extensive ones to be done in the future.

Dr. Miller would always explain exactly what he was going to do and what to expect after each surgery.

Some would be more difficult than others, but each one was done with the precision, as an Artist to his masterpiece.

The surgical transport teams were informed Aaron was never to be taken through those double doors without my kiss. This was my rule and they all understood completely. It had become a part of any surgery of Aaron's. It would be no different here; it was so hard to let him go through those doors…

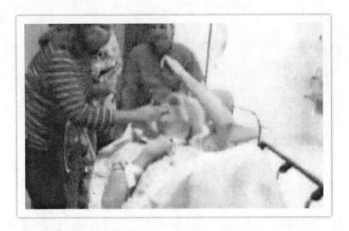

Dr. Miller was always very accurate in his estimates of how long Aaron would be in surgery. I would go into the out-patient surgical center, and the nurses would tell me where Aaron would be placed as soon as he was out of post-op. I would sit and wait for him to return.

It was my "job" to make sure Aaron had enough pain medication and a smooth transition from being under, and waking up. Aaron would wake up hard from being under anesthesia, if he was not given the sufficient amounts of an anti-anxiety medication.

There would be times when Aaron would wake up in the middle of Iraq, looking for his rifle, knife or Sergeant and afraid of being captured. Watching this and trying to calm his fears would put me in a panic. Several times Dr. Miller grabbed me by the shoulders to talk me down, while the anesthesiologist was working on the medications for Aaron. After every surgery, Aaron was dependent on me to make sure he had what was needed for pain and the transition.

Aaron soon returned after the first surgery, where Dr. Miller had prepared his nose and did some initial minimizing and straightening of his lips. Although the appearance was heart wrenching, we could begin to see the transformation Dr. Miller was envisioning for Aaron. Six days after surgery the stitches would be removed.

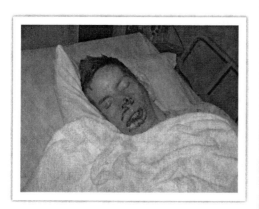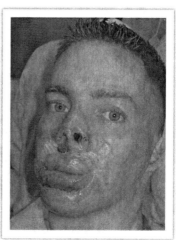

Dr. Miller would tell me, he would go to bed at night with Aaron's pictures laying out all around him on the bed as he studied Aaron's face. Years later, he would describe Aaron as the most challenging series of reconstructive surgeries he had ever done in his entire of career.

After numerous surgeries Dr. Miller was to the point of bringing down Aaron's forehead skin, to cover the cartilage which had been removed from what was left of his ears, to form a nose. This was one of the most astonishing procedures I had ever seen, and by far the hardest to watch Aaron go through. He would cut the forehead skin in the shape of a nose with the nostrils at Aaron's hairline. The flap of skin would be turned around, still attached just above the brow between his eyes, and placed over the cartridge. The blood flow would continue from the "Loop." After the blood supply was flowing from the stitched down sides of his new nose, then the loop would be removed.

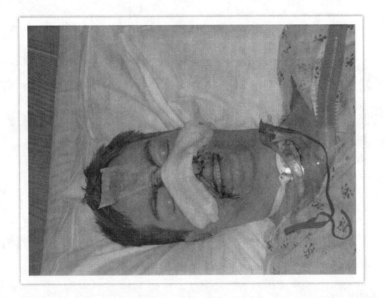

It was decided to leave the Tracheotomy tube in until all the surgeries were done. This would protect his scarred vocal cords from numerous re-intubations. It would be 3 years before they were ready to remove the tube and cut the binding scars that were causing Aaron's voice to be so harsh. Aaron was so strong; I was amazed at his resilience and humor after such a surgery.

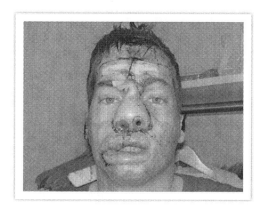

As hard as it was for me to watch, I couldn't imagine what Aaron must be going through. If it wasn't for the support of our Katz family, I'm not sure we would have gotten as far as we did.

Within a couple of days, we were over at Todd and Dana's with Ron and Maddie, watching a Lakers basketball game. Nobody could get as fired up over a basketball game as Maddie Katz. She was such a joy to be around.

Me, Aaron, Maddie & Ron Katz

Aaron would have a little fun with the "loop" between his eyes. He would be writing something and would expressionlessly place his pencil in the "noodle," (the nickname we gave to it) as a place to hold it. This little joke of his received odd looks and laughs, as he walked around with a pencil stretched across his eyes.

To Dr. Miller's astonishment and dismay, it appeared Aaron had inherited (from me) the ability to grow scar tissue at an unusual and alarming rate. Every time he would remove a scar it would reappear in a matter of days. This would be a constant problem in all of Aaron's future surgeries. As the months turned into years the surgeries continued. Dr. Miller was diligent in his strive for perfection, as one problem would arise after another. But, with each problem came a new solution…

The program was growing, as more and more disfigured wounded warriors were being brought into "Operation Mend." As the organization grew, more and more people from everywhere were being "infected." The development of office staff, within the UCLA Medical center, was growing by leaps and bounds to keep up with the needs of each patient and their families.

From the home of Todd and Dana Katz, and their love for the wounded warriors, another program was born called the *"Buddy Families."*

Dana would head up this new program and would find herself overrun with people, who had become "infected," wanting to volunteer their homes and friendship to a wounded warrior and their families. Los Angeles would become a second home for all who came from so far away. Every piece was still being developed and molded to best fit the needs of the patients who would be coming.

Aaron was the first patient, that made me the first Mom and we were fortunate to have Todd and Dana as the first *"Buddy Family."*

Todd and Dana Katz

Aaron and I counted our blessings at having Todd and Dana as our "Buddy Family." We became a part of their family, as they accepted us not only into their home but into their hearts.

We both easily came to love them, their four children, four dogs, nieces, nephews, parents, friends, siblings, cousins and anybody else who shared their lives, as a very special part of our family. They have taught us so much, by including us in their lives and the celebrations of their faith.

Our Buddy Family

With my entrance into the Katz family, the name situation had to be discussed. Aaron's wife was Diana, so that was out. I suggested Nana for everyone to call me, but was quickly rejected because Maddie Katz was called Nana by her grandchildren. Someone in the group suggested calling me "Nana Diana." It was perfect and I loved it. From that day to this I am "Nana Diana."

Wanting to ask so many questions of Dana, but not wanting to offend her in any way by my ignorance, I summoned the courage to ask if I could question her from a very uninformed perspective from time to time. She quickly answered me with, "You can ask me anything about anything and you will never offend me in any way." That eased my mind and opened the door to the beginning of a friendship which would grow deeper and deeper as we shared this journey together.

Every time Aaron and I would fly in for a surgery, we would stay an average of ten days. Todd and Dana would have us over to their home at least a couple of those nights and take us out to some of their favorite places on others. When we were having a casual night at their home, Todd was always the perfect bartender. The mix of Tequila with other ingredients would become my favorite. This would become known as the Toddarita. When we would go out,

Todd would give the waiter instructions on how to fix his special mixture. I know of at least one restaurant that put the drink on their menu as the "Toddarita."

We watched their four children growing up as they watched over Aaron's. On several occasions, Madeline Paige would spend the night before one of Aaron's surgeries with Dana and Todd. As soon as Dana volunteered to keep her for the very first time, Maddie reach out to her and was ready to stay. Just before her first birthday, Maddie took her first steps into the outstretched arms of Dana.

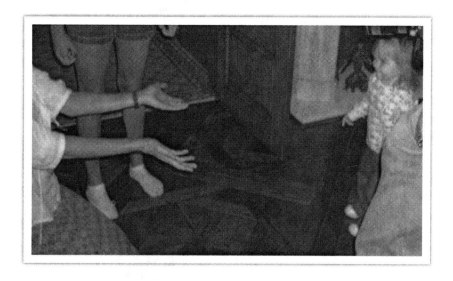

Dana was in tears while she cheered Madeline on to take another step. This moment was priceless.

Aaron and Diana were expecting their second child in September of 2008. This time they choose not to know the sex before giving birth. The deal had been with the first pregnancy they would find out the sex, so Diana could decorate the nursery. With the second,

Aaron wanted to have the feeling of not knowing until the moment the child was delivered.

Hunter Radek made his appearance on September 11th to an extremely happy father. While Aaron and I stood outside the hospital room, he raised his hands into the air and pulled them down while exclaiming to the world, "I have a Son!"

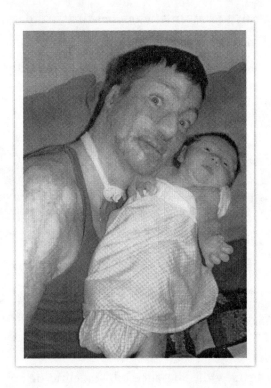

Aaron could hardly wait to take Hunter on his next trip to L.A. and show him off. Dana was waiting anxiously at the door and quickly reached out to hold the new baby boy. At the same time, Todd pulled me to the side and whispered in my ear, "Did they have him Circumcised?" I told him they had, and the furrow in his brow disappeared as he joined in the excitement of the moment.

This joyful time would be cut short. Only a few months later, on the next trip for another surgery, Aaron was served with divorce papers. Aaron fought for the custody of his two little ones and Diana agreed to avoid a public scandal. This time the damage to Aaron had been done on the inside and it was just as painful, if not more, as those wounds on the outside. Aaron now found himself in the position of being a single father of two very young children. Their welfare is the only thing that kept him going through everything still to be done.

The special bond we shared with all the Katz family was unique, and one I will always cherish. We shared so many pieces of our lives in the years that followed. They were always so willing to include us in their family events. I learned so much and knew so little...

There would be good times and tough ones to be shared between our families. When my sister passed and then my mother, I was greeted with open arms and words of comfort from Todd and Dana as well as all four of their children. Then when I was diagnosed with Breast Cancer, the love and compassion as well as the prayers brought me comfort and a sense of being surrounded by family.

There would be another member of our extended family to join us on our visits to California. Travis's younger brother, Ryan, was living in the L.A. area and would spend time with Aaron and me every time we were there, and became another son to me.

Ryan and Aaron

On one of our trips Aaron mentioned something, questioning how Maddie Katz was feeling. Aaron saw I was concerned and said, "I thought you knew." When I asked what was going on he told me she had been diagnosed with Pancreatic Cancer and was undergoing Chemotherapy. I was about to crumple with the grief I felt. Remembering my father's battle with this same cancer and how he suffered, over whelmed me when thinking of what was in store for this precious women.

Maddie Katz had become another mother to me. We never parted when she didn't hug me and tell me she loved me. More than once, this feisty little woman would shake her finger at me saying, "Make sure your husband takes good care of you when you get home!" She was always worried about my Lupus. Now Maddie Katz was the one who needed to be watched over. But, her spirit never left her as she faced this illness. She would laugh about wearing a wig she had been given by Dana's mother. "We have the same size heads," Maddie would say with laughter in her voice. I would see her on several occasions at Todd and Dana's home before she got too weak to come. I will never forget Maddie Katz...

Throughout the years our families have laughed together, cried for each other and lived for each other. Without the love and support of my Katz family, life would have been a whole lot less, in so many ways...

The Quilters Continue

The "gifting" of quilts continued in October of 2007, when the UCLA Medical Center and BAMC joined forces to start Operation Mend. Patti told her quilting group Aaron's story and the response was an over whelming, "What can we do?" This was the beginning of the "Quilts of Valor" to be made for each patient, who would follow in Aaron's path of recovery. Patti talked of her many years spent in the Army at the bedsides of soldiers. She knew what happened to them when they would come back. She makes these quilts in appreciation and respect for their service to our country.

Patti was born and raised in upstate New York, where quilting was a way of life. She learned how to sew as a child and her family has created quilts for generations. As a young woman she longed to be a doctor. Patti made a difficult choice to leave her family behind at the age of 17, for the Army during the Vietnam War. She underwent military training in 1964 at BAMC. The same hospital Aaron had arrived in back in May of 2005. Patti's Army service would take her to Iraq during the Persian Gulf War. She left active duty in 1993.

Patti meets with a dozen or so friends each Wednesday at a local fabric shop, to make quilts for U.S. soldiers returning home. These were some of the quilts Aaron had been given in the early days of his recovery at BAMC. She has lost track of the number of quilts she's created for military personnel over the years, but those of us who received one of these quilts will never forget the Patti's out there.

"I've been given the hands to mend and the heart to bring comfort and healing," she says, "We are a country at war. It will take a nation to heal."

Patti presented the first "Quilt of Valor" to Aaron, as the first patient of Operation Mend. Patti is holding Madeline Paige, Aaron's nine month old daughter and my third grandchild.

Love you Patti, always…

Someone had donated a building to their quilting community. They had outgrown the building they were in and wanted to have the opening ceremony when Aaron was in Los Angeles, so he could cut the ribbon. When they asked if I would like to attend, I was thrilled. I was so excited to have the chance to meet these people, who represented the quilting community who meant so much to me.

After the ribbon cutting ceremony concluded, a man and his wife came up to me while everyone enjoyed cookies and punch. The man, in his 60's, began in a soft and gentle voice to tell me a story about a quilt he made. This is what he had to say; about the making of this very special quilt.

Back in 2003, God told him to make a very special quilt. He was guided with the specifics of how the quilt was to be made, through his faith. It took him several months to complete the very intricate design. When he completed the final touches, The Lord told him, "I will let you know what to do with this quilt, when the time is come."

As the years passed he waited for word from above. This very talented Quilter took the quilt to fairs and quilting events to show it. It became an award-wining quilt. I suspect everyone could see the "Light" that shone from this very special piece of God's servants work…

When he heard I was coming with Aaron, he was told by The Lord, "Now." He knew instantly he was to give the quilt to me. When he told me his story and handed me this *"Quilt that God made for me,"* instantly the Holy Ghost Goose Bumps, started going all through me…

As I looked at the colors and the design, it took my breath away. It was such an amazing sight. It was truly a quilt made just for me. (The back cover of this book shows the colors of this beautiful quilt.) The quilt design is called "SUNBURST" by Jinney Beyer. What an appropriate name... It was pieced and quilted by God's obedient servant, Bill Horst of Los Angeles.

When we got back to our rooms at The Tiverton House, I laid the quilt out and took pictures of it, touched it and then prayed over it and its maker...

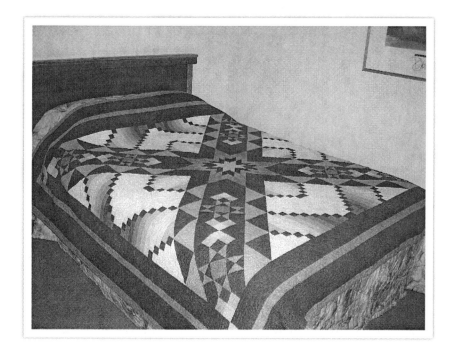

I felt so blessed by The Lord. He had this quilt made in 2003, which was two years before Aaron was injured, by this gifted Quilter of His. He knew how desperately I would need His comforting touch, all these years later...

I was amazed by the beauty and craftsmanship that had gone into the making of such a wonderful piece of art. God's work is always beyond what we can imagine.

This picture shows how every small piece of fabric was placed with such precision. Truly The Lord was guiding the hands that stitched and then embroidered this marvelous work of art. Thank you Lord for those blessed hands…

When I got home after that trip, I put the quilt on the back of my loveseat so I could show it to everyone. A few days later I was lying down on the loveseat; I reached up and pulled the quilt down on me. I felt as though angel's wings were wrapped all around me. With the peace that only The Lord can give, I feel asleep and rested as never before…

I am so grateful to all the Quilters who have touched our lives so completely. The

gift they give to all the wounded warriors and their families cannot be expressed

in mere words...

This wonderful quilt holds my family as well. Aaron is having his "snuggles" time with his two children.

This is something he does every night before bedtime.

And the blessings flow....

USO Awards Ceremony 2008

Aaron's call one night was exciting and a little funny. He was telling me about running into a friend of his from home in New York City, who was with the USO Liberty Bells. Heidi-Marie Ferren had told him about an award and asked if she could put his name in for consideration.

Aaron had been nominated to receive the "George Van Cleave Military Leadership Award" and for "The USO Marine of the Year." This would be the forty-seventh, USO OF METROPOLITAN NEW YORK, Armed Forces Gala & Gold Medal Dinner. It would be held on Monday, December 15, 2008 at Cipriani 42nd.

When he was chosen for this honor, everyone in the family could not have been more excited for him than I was. There would be a banquet and ceremony, with many attendees', who Aaron was looking forward to meeting or seeing again. But he had this one little problem.

Aaron's hair was falling out in a "U" shape at the front of his hairline. He had been receiving radiation treatments on the scar that remained down the center of his forehead. The scar was from the removal of skin to reconstruct a nose for him. The scar had been removed several times but continued to reappear. So these treatments were a last effort to kill the scar tissue and keep it from returning.

Of course, Aaron was at an earlier speaking engagement when he noticed the hair falling out in small patches just above the scar. Aaron decided the only way to handle the situation was to shave his head. No more problem…

When Aaron informed me he would be receiving the award as "The Marine of the Year," he also told me he would be the only one to have the honor of speaking for 3-4 minutes. I was excited and of course wanted to be there, but Aaron had told me I didn't need to come. There were a lot of things going on, and he knew I was having a very difficult time with my Lupus. I was on a lot of medications, Prednisone being the most dominate one. I didn't have to say anything, my family and friends could see how swollen and heavy I was from the high doses.

A few days before the USO Banquet and Award ceremony, I received a call from Aaron's father. Someone had given him a couple of tickets, but he would not be going. He asked if I wanted them and I jumped at the opportunity to see Aaron receive this award, and hear him speak. I called Jason, Aaron's older brother, and asked if he would like to escort me. Jason was thrilled at the opportunity to go.

We were going to New York City in three days. Jason rushed to get a Tux rented and I was going through my closet and pulled out a couple of dresses trying to decide. Jason had picked out a dress from a magazine he thought would look nice on me. I had purchased it months earlier for a time like this. That would be the dress I would wear.

All I knew was the place where the event would be held, so I called Cipriani 42nd and asked to talk to someone planning the USO event. A woman came on the phone, and when I identified myself as Aaron Mankin's mother she was excited to hear I would be coming.

I just wanted to make sure Jason and I would be seated at Aaron's table for the dinner. She was more than happy to give me the name and number of the man, at the USO, who was doing the seating arrangements. Then I asked if there was a hotel close by, so we could walk to the event, she informed me there was a hotel right across the street from them, but they were probably full. I called the hotel and made reservations without any problems. I called the man at the USO and he was enthusiastic and eager, as he began to think about me attending the ceremony.

They wanted to surprise Aaron with my presence. My airfare and hotel would be covered. I told him, I must see Aaron as soon as I got there. We had to give him time to catch his breath before he spoke. He agreed to meet Jason and me at the door, and we would search for Aaron among the crowd.

Jason and I boarded the plane for New York City. It was the first time either one of us had been there; we were both filled with anticipation. When we landed, we filled our bags with T-Shirts and other things from the "Big Apple." Then took a cab to the hotel and checked in.

We had a little over an hour to get ready to walk across the street. Jason and I changed into our formal attire, and got ready to go. Before we left, he called to make sure where to turn his tux in when the event was over. The place he had rented it from had an outlet just around the corner from where we were staying. This made it easier for him, so he didn't have to carry it back on the plane.

We were ready to step outside, and of course it was raining. By the time we had crossed the street; my hair was a mess and grew more frizzled with every drop of rain that touched it. Oh well, I really didn't care...

I was going to see my son receive an award and listen to him speak in front of a room full of very impressive people. What more could I ask for???

Jason opened the door of Cipriani's and we were in the most amazing world of:

The USO Gala

All photos of the USO were taken by Rob Rich

Jason and I started looking for Aaron as soon as we signed in at the front tables. It was so crowded; Jason leaned into my ear and said, "Do you know how much 'Big Brass' is in here." I had no idea; I just wanted to get to Aaron. I looked at Jason in his tux and thought how good he looked. Especially with those blue eyes...

Jason spotted a platform where people were mingling with Jon Voight, who was the Master of Ceremonies, and having their picture taken with him. The platform was about eight steps up. It was the perfect place to look through the crowd for Aaron. I went up the steps with my arm in Jason's; of course we had both grabbed a glass of Champaign as we passed through the crowd. Jason started looking around at the people on the platform, and began to point some of them out to me. There was a line of people waiting for their turn to have a picture taken. I wasn't interested in taking a picture and neither was Jason, but we both enjoyed meeting Jon Voight and some of the other guests.

We were standing on the platform when Jason spotted Aaron at the edge of the crowd. He was laughing and surrounded by other Marines. Jason stayed up on the platform while I went down to find Aaron in the area we had spotted him. If he moved, Jason could direct me to him.

I walked right up behind Aaron and tapped him on the shoulder. When he turned around, it was obvious he expected to see another fellow Marine. Total shook and surprise filled his face, as tears filled both our eyes; he grabbed me in his arms and held me. Aaron just kept saying, "Mom! Mom you're here! I'm so glad you are here!"

Then I told him Jason had come as well and pointed to the platform where he was standing, watching us. Aaron looked up at him with a huge grin on his face. Jason raised his glass as if to toast him. Aaron just laughed with surprise, while Jason looked surprisingly like "James Bond," leaning on the shiny, brass railing, in his tux, with a Champaign flute in his hand.

We mingled around the room, looking at everything. It was so wonderful to be there. Then we heard a call to find our tables and be seated, so we could be served dinner. The food was wonderful and the companionship was even better. Aaron was talking to everyone and barely had a chance to eat his dinner. Soon he would be called up front. Our table was on the isle about four rows from the front.

While everyone was eating and talking, I took a peek at the booklet of events and turned to the page that showed Aaron's profile. The picture was an older one which did not reflect his most recent reconstructive surgeries. The picture brought back a flood of memories… I closed the book and concentrated on how happy Aaron was now, here, in this moment of time. I was so grateful just to be here and share this experience with him.

Travis Coursey was there with Aaron to make sure he was where he needed to be, when he needed to be there. Aaron was still having difficulty with short term memory loss and would lose track of time. He relied on Travis a lot during the years to come. Travis didn't have time to eat much of his dinner either. He spent most of the banquet time near the stage checking to see when they would need Aaron to come up there. Soon, Travis was at Aaron's side to walk him to the front of the stage where everyone was gathering to go on as their turns came.

As Travis and Aaron were standing up to leave the table Aaron turned to me and said, "I love you mom, I can't imagine you not being here." Then, with great joy and excitement they rushed off to the stage.

Jason was getting restless and started roaming, around the room, to see all the people who were there. Jason was, and is, an avid reader of history. Especially, reading and watching documentaries which accurately portray our countries Heroes, during conflicts and wars. He admires his brother and counts him as one of our nations *"Greatest War Heroes."*

Every so often Jason would come hurrying back to the table to let me know who was there. I was glad to see him in the same room with so many people he truly admired.

The ceremony is beginning; a hush falls over the crowed room.

First the Presentation of the Colors, the National Anthem

and all the dignitaries from the USO and other organizations, who support the USO, spoke.

Then it was Jon Voight's turn to begin the introductions after his initial remarks.

Before I knew it Aaron was being introduced, he walked up the nine or ten steps to the stage and bowed his head as the ribbon, with the Gold Coin was placed around his neck.

The George Van Cleave Military Leadership Award is the USO's way of publicly honoring and thanking them for their outstanding commitment, exceptional service, sacrifice and achievements of individuals who have shown extraordinary dedication to their country.

Aaron was obviously very humbled by this award. General David H. Petraeus was standing next to Aaron, watching with pride and as you can see, GREAT JOY…

What a wonderful sight as everyone stood and applauded. As I stood, I was crying at the sight of this honor given to my son. I was so proud of him, and I truly appreciated the way this room full of people were honoring Aaron.

I knew he was about to speak, so I kept praying as he stood still waiting for people to be seated. After a few moments, Aaron went over to the podium and began by thanking everyone while Jon Voight stood at the side of the stage.

While Aaron spoke, he mentioned family and how important the families of the service members were, especially to the recovery of those who were wounded. Then he gave me our sign, following Carol Burnett's lead, as he touched his ear meaning, "Love you, Mom."

Aaron spoke for a couple of minutes, always with his right hand on his throat to the tube in his airway. All of us around him were used to the way he spoke and didn't think about the way he would stop while speaking to catch his breath. It wasn't a noticeable interruption in his speaking.

As Aaron continued his speech, he put his hand up to his mouth and took a step back. He held up a finger and gestured to just give him a second. Aaron was a little emotional, talking about how much family means to him. I started praying again. As my head was bowed I felt two hands grab me by each arm, and lift me out of my chair.

These two men carried me; my feet were not touching the floor, to the bottom of the stage. I looked up, and Jon Voight grabbed my arm and carried me up the stairs and onto the stage. I hurried over to Aaron and just hugged him while we both sobbed…

I wasn't aware of anything or anyone but Aaron as he buried his face even deeper in my hair. Then all of a sudden, my arm was being pulled by someone. I looked up and saw Jon Voight with his hand grasping my arm, pulling me away from Aaron. He pushed me toward the podium and said, "Speak."

I found myself in front of a very silent crowd as they watched this drama unfold before them. All I could think of was to tell the story of when I first got to Aaron, in San Antonio. He had been speaking about family so that would fit right in. I turned and checked, to see Jon and Aaron embracing, so I began.

My story: "Aaron was talking about family. When I got to Aaron at Brooke Army Medical Center, at 3:00 in the morning, he had been out of surgery for a short time."

I looked around again and watched Jon and Aaron before continuing.

Everything seemed to be under control and Jon and Aaron were laughing. I went on with my story...

"The Nurse came out to talk to his brother, Jason and me to prepare us for what we would see. I just wanted to get to him, and she took us back to his room and opened the door. Aaron did not have any bandages on his face. The scars from the heat had not yet begun to show. I leaned down to his ear and whispered, "Aaron momma's here." His heart rate rapidly increased and his blood pressure rose. The nurse looked at me and said he knew I was there. That is what you all do when you help the USO go out to our service members. You are saying, Home is here."

I never felt the presence of Aaron behind me while I spoke...

I turned back into Aaron's arms and began sobbing again. The crowd of people were on their feet applauding and crying with us.

Jon stood back and held a hand up signaling us to just stand there a moment.

As you can see I had completely lost it while Aaron was now in complete control…

As we were walking off the stage, Jon Voight looked at me grinning and said, "Perfect." That was my Oscar moment.

I continued back to our table while Aaron and Travis stayed at the bottom of the stage with the others to be honored. Aaron was standing with General Patreus having his picture taken.

I got back to the table and everyone started coming up to me expressing their emotions at what they had just seen. Jason was staying by my side to make sure I was alright. Then Aaron came running down the aisle to our table. He came up to me and told me General Petreus wanted me to have this. Aaron put his hand in mine and slipped me a coin. My first military Challenge Coin! From General Petreus! I still cannot believe that night.

Oh, Travis had a good time too…

Hand Surgery

On one of our trips to Los Angeles, Aaron had several appointments as well as a minor surgery on his left hand. His right hand was more disfigured from the fire and had been partially amputated. It appeared to me, to have 4th degree burns, because of the bone damage it had sustained. *Operation Mend made* it possible for not only Aaron to receive the best medical care, but also for myself as his caregiver to be with him during all of his surgeries at little or no expense.

Because this was a minor surgery, Aaron had accepted a speaking engagement in Virginia. It was a fund raiser, Golf Tournament and Auction on behalf of "The Fallen Heroes Fund." Aaron would fly out after his release from the hand surgeon, Dr. Azari and from Dr. Timothy Miller.

Over the years the relationship with Dr. Miller had become one of not only patient and doctor, but also one of friends, even father to son and mentoring from one war veteran to another, dealing with PTSD.

Dr. Miller had become so much more to me as well. I was so grateful for his relationship with Aaron and the way he had made it a personal one. However, he had taken me in as well. Dr. Miller had spent a lot of time dealing with one very frightened mother after several surgeries, especially when Aaron would have trouble coming out from under the anesthesia. This was very difficult in the beginning, until the right combination of medications had been established to help him through the transition period.

I cannot count the times Dr. Miller would say to me over the years, "Now Mom, calm down, let's treat the patient." With his simple but direct way, he would put me at ease and assure me that he understood. After one surgery while we stood outside Aaron's room, he even shared with me his own experience with PTSD after returning from Vietnam. He understood exactly what Aaron was going through.

Aaron and I had been invited on several occasions to his home for dinner, and to enjoy not being in a clinical setting and to share his famous grilled burgers. Dr. Miller's wife was a gracious and caring person whom we came to love as well.

On one of these visits with them, I had bent down and picked up a pine cone from under one of their trees. Aaron and I were on our way back to The Tiverton House, but Dr. Miller pleaded with me to take all the pine cones, *PLEASE!!!* I assured him all I needed was one.

The purpose of taking the pine cone was to have Aaron's two children plant it in my yard next spring, then see it magically grow into a Christmas tree when they came during the holiday's.

So often "Daddy" went away to have surgery and on some of these occasions, Aaron would bring the children with him. They would go to his appointments with Dr. Miller and they knew he was the doctor who was making daddy better. The Christmas tree they planted in my front yard is from their friend, Dr. Miller's home.

Dr. Miller had a hard time keeping a straight face with Aaron's quick wit.

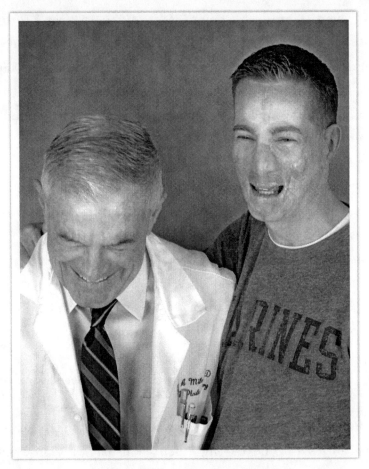

Photo by Michelle Van Vliet

Aaron had an appointment with the best hand surgeon in the country, Dr. Azari, the day before surgery. They agreed to do surgery on his left hand that would allow almost full function. After the surgery,

Aaron's hand was bandaged in a way which rendered it completely useless.

While Aaron was recuperating after this surgery, we were invited by Michael Broderick, a retired Marine and actor, to visit Gary Sinise on the set of CSI: NY. This would be the high light of this trip to Los Angeles for me. I was and am a major fan, and watched this series on the reruns as well as the current weekly shows.

Michael picked us up and we headed to the set where they were getting ready to shot a scene for the up-coming series. Michael took us to Gary's trailer and after banging on the door a couple of times, Gary opened the door with a crooked grin on his face and invited us in. We sat there and talked as Aaron answered Gary's questions about how he was injured and he shared with us some of the things he was doing to help raise awareness and funds for wounded warriors. His Lt. Dan Band would be playing the following week, but we would be gone by then and wouldn't be able to get the back stage tour Gary had offered. Hopefully, in the near future we would.

Gary wanted to show us around the set and we were having a great time walking and talking as he would take us from one place to another. He would suggest photo shoots at various places to show off the set and we loved the opportunity.

We would see some of the outside backdrops for the show and then we went inside. Gary walked us through some of the sets and then was told he needed to get dressed for the next shoot. He had someone else take us through some of the inside offices, but before he left us Gary spent a little more time just talking and listening.

Gary is a committed supporter of our troops and spends as much time as possible giving back to those who serve this country. In 2010 he would establish the "Gary Sinise Foundation" dedicated to honoring and serving our defenders.

Gary doesn't just talk the talk; he has dedicated himself to walking the walk...

Gary left and Aaron, Michael and I continued to roam around the sets. Aaron was especially interested in the display case on the wall in Detective Mac Taylor's office. It contained some of the "Coins" Gary had been given from members of the Military. Challenge coins are usually given by a high ranking Officer all the way up to the President. They are given in recognition of exemplary performance and outstanding mission accomplishment, yet at the same time, challenging them to continue to achieve. It is an honor to receive one and it is usually done in a very discreet way, usually from palm to palm in the course of a handshake.

Gary joined us again and took us back to where the scene was about to be shoot with John Larroquette. We sat in those high studio chairs and watched as they went through the scene three times and then they were finished and John rushed out as Gary thanked him for coming. We then went back through the offices; Gary wanted to make sure we had seen everything.

Before we left, Aaron was sitting at the desk on the set, looking at the bandaged hand and wondering how this was going to affect his travel and speaking plans. With his right hand as disfigured as it was, Aaron had adapted to it and could manage a few basic things. But, buttons, clasps, and many small functions were beyond its ability, without the help of his good left hand. This caused a major problem when it came to Aaron's speaking engagement. Without the use of his hands, how was he going to get into his Dress Blues?

So, the only solution was for me to go with him to Virginia. It was a beautiful Country Club, Golf Tournament and fund raising weekend. It was autumn, and the trees were just beginning to change colors. While the guests spent the day golfing, I walked and took pictures of the beautiful landscape, with its flowers and trees in the rolling hills. It was beautiful.

This event was hosted by the Tiger Wood Foundation. Aaron was speaking on behalf of the Intrepid Fallen Heroes Fund which would be the beneficiary of the night's proceeds. Aaron spoke at the dinner with his usual humor and captivated everyone.

After the auction was over, one of the guests and his wife came over to our table carrying a large basket filled with Channel products. They very generously presented me with the gift which left me speechless and grateful for their generosity to me and the fund.

It was a wonderful distraction from the hospital atmosphere we had been used to.

The weekend was over before we knew it and we were off to the airport to head home. As Aaron and I were sitting in our seats on the plane waiting to take off, he reached over and took my hand. He raised it to his lips and kissed the back of my hand. As I looked in his eyes I could see the meaning and remembrance so well...

When my children went to school, a tradition was started between me and them. Each morning before they left, I would kiss the back of their hands. This would leave an impression with my lipstick, of my kiss, that they would take with them. It meant I was with them, even when we were apart...

Photo by Michelle Van Vliet

This time, Aaron was returning the message...

Another Crisis

2009 was a difficult time for Aaron, as well as a very disappointing one for all of us who loved him so much. Besides the continuing surgeries, he was dealing with the end of his marriage. I saw him slipping further and further into himself, and away from me and everyone who cared about him.

I was receiving phone calls, text messages and e-mails, asking if I could get in touch with Aaron to have him return their messages. He was hiding in his own small world of his two children, which he had custody of, and the house that had once been a home. The house only served as a reminder to him of the ugliness of what had gone on inside, while he was away. But, he was focusing on his children's needs and the comfort of living in "their home" even though their mother had moved out earlier that year.

At first, Aaron would answer my calls or texts. As the weeks passed, the communication between Aaron and anyone else became less and less. I kept thinking it was something I had done that was responsible for him not returning my calls. But, when I talked to other people who were having the same trouble with Aaron not responding to them, I realized it wasn't just me. I became very frightened by Aaron's behavior.

Aaron and I were still flying out to Los Angeles for his surgeries every few weeks. But, I was getting the information and schedules from the *Operation Mend* office rather than from Aaron. They began calling me to make sure we were coming. I knew he felt bad about how he was conducting himself. He even felt he was letting his friends and family down. He was so overwhelmed; he would let his messages back up to the point where no one could even leave him a new one. The message box was full and closed.

As soon as we would arrive in Los Angeles, Aaron would put on his "Aaron Persona," so everyone would think everything was business as usual. On one trip when we arrived at the airport, it was the first time we had spoken in several weeks. As Aaron gave me a hug he whispered in my ear, "Mom, I'm in trouble." I knew exactly what he meant and I was determined to do whatever it took to help him.

When we got back into our rooms at The Tiverton House, Aaron and I sat on one of the beds and talked for hours. Every time he would say something in a negative way I would suggest he think of it in a positive light. He needed to find the excitement rather than becoming overwhelmed by whatever was happening. This was the way Aaron had always approached everything in his life, he just needed to be reminded of the part of him that seemed to have vanished.

Aaron went back to his room to get ready for dinner with Todd and Dana, and I gave Dana a call. She would let Todd know, so he would be aware of Aaron's need to talk to somebody. The next morning Aaron had several appointments in preparation for surgery the following day. I called Dana to ask about Todd and Aaron talking the night before, when they had disappeared for a while.

Aaron had opened up to him, and Todd had made sure Aaron had an appointment that morning with someone who specialized in PTSD (Post Traumatic Stress Disorder). Dana believed this doctor would be a good fit for Aaron and would be able to help him with everything he was dealing with, but it would take time.

With the holiday's approaching, I was still having trouble getting through to Aaron on any kind of regular bases. As the time between trips to California grew further apart, it was easy for Aaron to slip into his, non-responsive mode.

Just before Thanksgiving I noticed some changes in my right breast and contacted my doctor. He immediately sent me for several tests. The biopsy showed Cancer in the two lymph nodes as well as the tissue samples from the breast itself. There was also a mass in my right hip joint that was causing pain when I walked. The mass was visible on the scans, but the doctors were not able to determine if this too was malignant.

I choose not to tell anyone until after Christmas. Even with this diagnoses, I just was not worried or scared about what would happen. I was still in that "Bubble of Peace" from The Lord, which had been a constant part of my life. I had seen so many injured and disfigured wounded warriors that whatever was ahead of me could not come close to what they were enduring, including Aaron…

After the holidays, I had some phone calls to make to my children and family. My mother was in the hospital and on one of my visits I told her about the cancer. I told everyone except Aaron. He wouldn't return my calls and he was back in that hiding state. I tried for several days, but there were no replies.

Jason decided to send Aaron a text telling him to call me. His message was, "It's bad." Aaron called and after a minute of chatting I told him what was going on and he started sobbing. I kept saying I was sorry and his reply was, "How am I supposed to feel about my mother dying." I tried to calm him by telling him I wasn't dying, yet we both continued to sob, me for my baby and my baby for me…

After the phone call in January, Aaron was answering and calling on a regular basis. I had a mastectomy in February and was out of the hospital in just a few days. Don was so strong, he never allowed himself to show any fear in front of me. He waited on me hand and foot. Don accompanied me to every appointment and after the surgery he insisted on seeing everything. He would help with the changing of bandages and the emptying of drains. Don was not going to allow me to hide from what was taking place in my body. We had learned immediately after the surgery they had removed a five centimeter mass and four more lymph nodes; all had cancer cells in them. This was not a good sign.

I had an appointment with the Oncologist two weeks after surgery to hear the pathology report and the plan for treatment. The night before, I called my prayer warriors (my children) and asked that we all pray a very specific prayer, "There is not a Cancer cell in my body."

As Don and I were leaving to go to this appointment, I walked by the door to our spare bedroom. I noticed a white envelope on the dresser and so I went in and picked it up. It was from the Pathologist with the report from my surgery. I stuck it in my purse and out the door we went.

When Don and I arrived at the Oncologists office we were taken back to the usual exam room, and waited for the doctor to appear. In just a few minutes, he came hurriedly in the room explaining he did not have the report from the Pathologist yet. I told him I had it and handed it to him as he replied, "Oh good."

The doctor opened the envelope and asked if I had a pen, as he began to read. I handed him one of those bank pens, which everyone has in their possession, and watched as he began to study the report. He started backing up and put the pen in his mouth until he was leaning against the wall on the other side of the room. He continued to study the document and bent one knee, raising his foot up on the wall. The doctor muttered to himself, "This is very unusual." Then he raised his eyes and looked me straight in mine and said, "There is not a cancer cell in your body."

Those words made my heart rejoice, my eyes water, my skin fill with "Holy Ghost goose bumps" as I praised Him for answered prayer. How marvelous it was to hear the same words we had prayed, spoken back to us so precisely. One more "God-Incident," definitely...

The doctor said he would like to do three or four rounds of Chemotherapy, just in case. I went along with what he was suggesting and scheduled my first round, along with the surgery to have the "Port" put into my chest, just below the collar bone. They would use this "Port" to administer the mix of drugs the Oncologist prescribed.

The next week I was in the room, with so many others, having the drugs hung on a pole and placed in the Port. My daughter, Sarah and her husband, James Cunningham were with me. Sarah looked at me with teary eyes and said, "Mom, you are just so strong." I wasn't at all, but it was good to hear I was fooling those around me. I told Sarah I was too vain about my hair, so I thought The Lord would allow all my hair to fall out. She laughed and nodded her head.

About a week after my first treatment I was confronted by one of my children. I was informed God does not do "Just in case, Miracles." I had to agree and on my next visit to the Oncologist when asked if I wanted to do anymore treatments, I simply relied "No." He said alright, and that was that.

There was one more side effect I was unprepared for. It was the effect the Chemotherapy drugs had on my Immune System. They had put my Lupus in remission and I had more energy, after the effects of the one treatment wore off, than I had felt in years. I was able to go way down on the Prednisone dosage which caused a drop in the swelling of my body. The weight dropped off and I was back to the size I had been all my life.

Bald and praising The Lord all the way to the wig stores!!! Oh, I almost forgot, the mass in my hip had unexplainably disappeared...

Photo by Michelle Van Vliet

April 2010

2010 had started off with such a shock for Aaron when confronted with my mortality; he opened every door possible for me to be with him. He knew I would cherish the opportunities to listen to him speak, meet new friends and spend time with him.

In March, Aaron asked if I would like to attend the Marine Parents Conference in New Orleans. He would be the keynote speaker at the Saturday night dinner and had spoken at the previous two conferences. It was to be in New Orleans on April 16th through the morning of the 18th. I jumped at the chance, when he told me I could tell all the "Mommy Stories" I wanted.

Aaron would tell me, as we were about to enter an event, "Now remember, you're Arm Candy." This was to let me know, I was not to embarrass him by telling any "Mommy Stories" to his friends and acquaintances. I understood these were business gatherings and it would not be appropriate for me to bring up such personal things. But, as his mother, this was a very hard thing not to do.

I had finished with Chemotherapy and the reconstruction surgeries by the dates of the conference, so I was eager to get out and enjoy some time away. I had purchased the first of many wigs to cover my bald head, and some new clothes to fit my shrinking figure. To say the least, I was really looking forward to this weekend.

When April rolled around my mother was not doing well, and my oldest son, Jason, his wife and I would take turns staying with her at the Condo she owned in Oklahoma City. She needed 24/7 care to get around and it took all three of us to help her with all her needs. On April 12th she asked me to bring the Bible I studied from with me the next day, when I came. I did as she asked and arrived the next morning with my Bible. Jason and his wife had some business to take care of and would be gone most of the day.

Mom stayed in her recliner most of the time, and even slept in it. The positioning of it was more comfortable for her than a bed, and her legs had become heavy and useless. She talked about how she had been praying, for the last two weeks, for The Lord to take her.

I sat next to her recliner and opened my Bible to various scriptures describing what Heaven is like. After a couple of hours, Mom asked me to pray with and for her. As we prayed asking The Lord to grant my Mother's request of freedom from her crippled body, mom asked that I be blessed for all I had done. I was crying and so was Mom, then she said she was tired and wanted to take a nap. Mom fell asleep very quickly after the prayer, and never woke up...

My Mother (78) journeyed from this life to the next on an answered prayer, on April 14, 2010.

She had longed to join my Dad (Kenneth Gene Lindsey), sister (Cheryl Lindsey Preston) and brother (Keith Alan Lindsey), as well as all who had gone before her.

I had expected when this time came, my brother and sister would be there to help. But, they both had already gone. I was left alone to make the arrangements. One person told me I was an orphan now, and that is exactly how I felt.

When I called Aaron to let him know Mom had passed on and to tell him I couldn't go to the Marine Parents Conference. He was shaken by the loss, but was not going to accept that I wasn't going to go. We would just fly in a day late and then return for the funeral. I just didn't see how it was possible; I had so many things to do, and arrangements to make.

I sat down with Mom a couple of years before and gone through an arrangement brochure. Everything was written down, so when it came time to meet with the Funeral Director to give him all the information it was right there. I didn't have to do very much and after picking out the Casket and all that, I left some of the other things to Sarah and Jason to finalize. The soonest the Funeral Home could schedule the ceremony was the following Tuesday. That left the weekend open and distraction was welcomed. I called Aaron with the schedule and agreed to go with him to New Orleans.

I was frantically packing for the trip, changing my mind about what to wear every few minutes and taking out what was packed and replacing them. I was working in a fog and needed to leave for the airport. I left in plenty of time to check in and board, but once again trouble was in front of me.

As I was approaching the airport parking areas, my car began to swerve. It was as if someone or something had their hands on the steering wheel turning it hard, from one side to the other. I was trying with all my strength, to straighten the course of the car. But every time I would pull the wheel to one side it would be pulled, with a hard jerk, in the opposite direction. I was traveling at 30mph and swerving from one side, of the three lane street, to the other.

There was a taxi behind me watching and a man with the airport roads department, on an adjoining road, also looking on as I was obviously out of control. After what seemed like a lifetime, my car did a complete turn around and slammed against the high curb of the outside lane facing the oncoming traffic. All the approaching vehicles stayed back, out of the way until my car stopped, before continuing around me. The taxi stopped to see if I was alright, and the man with the airport came over quickly as well.

Everyone agreed something on my steering mechanism had broken, causing me to lose control. I was in that car and knew there was a battle going on, but trying to explain it would have been confusing. The man in the taxi needed to go, to catch his flight, so the man with the airport told him to go. He would tell the Police when they arrived, what happened.

I was watching the time, afraid I was going to miss my flight. In an attempt to get things moving, I called AAA for a tow to the dealer while we waited for the Officer to arrive on the scene. The driver side tires and wheels on my car were demolished. When the Officer arrived, the man and I told our stories and I explained I really needed to catch my flight. As the Officer was writing his report the tow truck arrived, he looked at me with a grin and asked if I had already called for a tow. This officer was definitely sent from above. He finished the papers so the truck could clear the road of my severely damaged car, and then drove me to my airline.

I checked my bags and made it through security, then headed for the gate where the airplane was boarding. Walking briskly down the corridor, I felt someone come up next to me from behind. I looked up and there was the kind Police Officer holding my sun glasses saying, "You forgot something." We laughed and I thanked him for everything as he told me to go catch my flight. I would meet Aaron at the airport in New Orleans; we were landing at about the same time.

As soon as we enter the JW Marriot Hotel, Aaron was surrounded by friends and fellow Marines he had served with. We proceeded to the registration table, picked up our name tags and greeting bags filled with all kinds of things. I would check this out later. This was the third time Aaron had been a speaker for this annual event, and this time he would be the keynote speaker at the Saturday night dinner. Everyone had already fallen in love with his charismatic personality.

When Aaron went to check in and get our rooms, he found we had been placed on different floors and very far apart. Aaron told the woman at the desk, we had requested our rooms be next to each other or at least close. She said she was sorry, but there wasn't anything she could do we would have to stay with the rooms we had been assigned. Aaron and I stepped away from the desk to talk this over and I asked him to let me handle it, he gave me a nod and I went back to the young woman behind the desk.

I told her the room assignments were not acceptable, and I would like to talk to the manager. She went into an office and came out with the explanation he was on his way, and would be with me in just a minute. As Aaron and I stood there, the manager came walking rather hurriedly from down a side hall. I explained the situation, and he went behind the desk and to the computer. After checking the room situation out he approached us, with keys in hand and said, "I think this will suit your needs much better and thank you for your patients."

When Aaron and I opened the door to our sweet "Suite," we were astonished by the luxurious, two level, multi-roomed accommodations. We would be very comfortable and Aaron agreed to always let me handle any "room changes" in the future. Several of his buddies would come by over the course of our stay to admire our "Suite," and give Aaron a hard time about roughing it.

After unpacking we went down to the rooms where people were milling around and coming out of some of the workshops that were taking place. I met so many wonderful people who had been through some of the same experiences I had. There was an instant bond with several mothers and we agreed to meet at the reception before dinner, and share more of our stories. After checking out all that was going on, Aaron suggested we go back upstairs and get ready for the nights activates.

Back in our rooms, I had a chance to look over the folder with the agenda and all the speakers' biographies. After the welcoming page was Aaron's, with the picture which had become a trademark on most articles being published.

On the next page was Russ Meade, who would be the Master of Ceremonies for the night. Russ and Aaron had served together in Iraq in the Public Affairs office, and had visited us at BAMC several times while Aaron was recovering. They would meet at various functions through the years. Their bond was a strong one they both would always share. It was good to see Russ again earlier that day.

Russ spent eight years in the Marines, and then re-enlisted again to deploy to Iraq in 2004. He founded *Operation Freedom Ballot* when he returned to the states. Russ wanted to honor those who had fallen, by giving the Gold Star families an official ballot from the first democratic election in Iraq's history. Freedom, their Heroes had paid the ultimate price for, was placed in their hands...

It was time to head down to the reception and meet the people Aaron had grown so close to. When we walked into the reception room heads turned to look at the tall, young Marine in his Dress Blues.

There just isn't anything like the Marine Corps Dress Blues, with the Blood Stripe running down the length of the slacks. Although I may be a little prejudice, but Aaron looked especially impressive in them, and he had earned the right to wear them proudly.

Meeting Tracy Della Vecchia was not only an inspiration but a delight. She is the founder and heart behind this dedicated organization. The mother of a Marine, who has served three tours in Iraq, gives her the insight it takes to run an organization that has continued to grow in its outreach programs at an astonishing rate. Stemmed from a mother's love, Marine Parents has become one of the most successful efforts in helping not just Parents and Marines, but all who love them.

One of Aaron's close friends came in and headed straight for him, Peter Menzies; his company, Covert Threads, had donated the greatest quality military socks ever, which had been put in our goody bags. I still wear them and we spent time talking about the sock industry. I had bought socks for the Sam's Clubs for years, so we were talking shop about people we both knew.

After a few minutes, Pete would tell me about the relationship he had with Aaron. He felt within minutes of meeting Aaron, several years earlier, he knew him better than people he had known for years. There was an instant connection between them and he admired the open, authentic person Aaron was. He said he could look in his eyes and see right down to his soul. I had heard this description before and understood completely. That was "The Aaron Connection."

I saw one of the ladies I had met earlier, Dee Mills, and she was headed my way and I headed toward her. As we met, she began to tell me her story as a Marine Mom. Her son did not come home. Yet her convections to always be a Marine Mom were clear. She was proud of what her son had given his life for, and I do mean given. Not taken, but given so the Iraqi people could have a chance at the freedom we so often take for granted. I stopped  and considered what if the phone call I had received had been one of loss instead of injury. I have the utmost, heartfelt gratitude and respect for the mothers of those whose sons or daughters did not make it back home alive.

In a conversation a year or so later, Aaron told me how he had never been hugged so hard as by the Gold Star mothers. I thought as he told me this, they were imagining hugging their own child as they held mine. I am so grateful for each hug I receive from Aaron and will never take one of them for granted...

The dinner bell began ringing and instructions were coming for us to all move into the dining room. Aaron had checked out the tables earlier so he guided me to the one with our place cards. Just as Russ opened the gates of Heaven with his prayer of blessing over the meal, I felt as though I had been thumped in the head by God himself. The clarity of the past few days was overwhelming...

I heard these words as clear as if He were standing next to me; "It's not you, it's Aaron." The message was explaining to my soul that the "accident" at the airport, along with several other incidents, were an attack against Aaron not me. If I had been hurt or killed, it would have changed the course that Aaron was on. Evil was trying to alter the plan for Aaron, by attacking the ones he loved.

I couldn't control myself when my eyes were instantly opened, and I reached over and touched Aaron's knee during the prayer. He shushed me with his head bowed, but as soon as the prayer was over I told Aaron what had been revealed to me. He listened intently, yet not quite understanding the full extent of what I was saying. We would have a lengthier conversation later. Once the attacks on the family were revealed, it was just a matter of prayer to stop them and protect the family and friends whom Aaron held so dear.

Toward the end of the dinner it was Aaron's turn to speak. He touched all in the room with the words only Aaron has, and I am sure there was a larger purpose for him being at this conference than I may ever know.

But God knew, and intervened at every turn to make sure His will was done...

The Fallen Heroes Fund

After we left the Marine Parents conference in New Orleans, Aaron received a request from the Fallen Heroes Fund to come to New York in June. Aaron had committed to a one year contract with them to speak and help raise funds. I had attended some of these speaking engagements and Travis had accompanied Aaron on some as well. For this occasion, Aaron would be surrounded by friends and others he had met while serving as a spokesperson aboard the USS Intrepid.

This request for Aaron's presence turned out to be one that would be talked about for some time and was covered in the press from here to as far away as South Africa. Prince Harry was coming to New York on a three day trip and one of his stops would be on board the USS Intrepid.

The photographers had a field day watching the Prince and the Marine, as they obviously enjoyed each other's company from the moment they met.

The stories between the two could only be imagined and was sure to hold comments that are shared only among the ranks of those who have served their countries.

Aaron and Prince Harry shared a common bond. They had both gone to war and both served in Iraq. Their experiences had been completely different and yet the bond of "brothers in arms" was felt by both.

Prince Harry was very interested in the metals and all their meanings, which were a part of Aaron's military history. Aaron told of the tradition and meaning of each medal as he held a wounded finger over the tube in his throat.

They were both able to talk frankly and honestly about how those who were returning from war were being received by their countries. Aaron was very interested in how the U.K. handled their wounded when they returned from war. Prince Harry listened intently as Aaron questioned his countries medical response for their returning wounded warriors and how the United States had been responding to ours.

Then it was Aaron's turn to listened, as Prince Harry explained how their wounded warriors were treated when they returned from war. He also told Aaron how the health care system in his country worked in regards to all its citizens.

This exchange was one that Aaron will never forget and I'm sure Prince Harry will always remember the young Marine, who had so many questions along with some insight into how a nation should support their heroes.

By the time the afternoon came to a close both Aaron and Prince Harry realized they had even more in common than they had suspected through the conversations about military service.

They are both the youngest sons to a mother, Diana, and a father, Charles.

Stand Up For Heroes

Aaron continued to invite me along on some of his speaking engagements, as the year of my recovery continued. He was also still having surgeries at UCLA Medical Center for his facial reconstruction. I would accompany Aaron on these trips, as always. When it came to surgery, I still could not let him go through those doors without giving him, one more kiss.

In October, Aaron asked if I wanted to attend the *Bob Woodruff Foundations* fund raiser in New York City. I was excited at the invitation and accepted it eagerly. He told me a little about what to expect, but I must say I was overwhelmed by the reception I received.

The *Stand Up For Heroes* auction and fund raiser was to be held on November third, with a reception and dinner the night before. When Aaron and I entered the reception that night, he was eager to introduce me to Lee and Bob Woodruff. I was a little nervous. We had watched Bob's recovery when he was the victim of a road side bomb in Iraq, only eight months after Aaron. They would share a lot in the years as they both recovered and got to know each other. I was happy to have this opportunity to see the friendship and bond between them.

Stand Up For Heroes is a clearinghouse of sorts. The donations they raise are used to Grant and Fund veterans support organizations. Each one who receives monies from them is held accountable, so each one who gives will know their dollars are being used wisely.

The room was crowded as Aaron and I entered, and I followed him through the crowd with my hand in his arm as always. He introduced me to people he had met in the two previous years he had been a guest of theirs.

Then he saw Lee surrounded by a group of people and Aaron began to move in her direction. We came up behind her and Aaron touched her shoulder as Lee turned toward him. She immediately grabbed Aaron and hugged him with great pleasure at seeing him. He pulled me in and introduced me to Lee. Before Aaron could get another word out she put her arm around me, pulling us closer so we could hear each other over the noise of the crowd. Lee told me, "I know we're not supposed to have favorites, but I just love Aaron." Aaron was blushing.

Lee turned her head, searching for Bob in the crowd. When she spotted him, she started calling out for him to join us. Lee introduced me to Bob, who swept me up and gave me a hug making me feel so special. He said he was going to walk me down the Red Carpet the next night. I was speechless. I really didn't know exactly what that even meant. All I knew was it would be an honor I would cherish for the rest of my life.

Lee and I stayed in a huddle talking and sharing, with tears in our eyes for each other's struggles. When Lee looked at me and said, "We are sisters." Simply and plainly, she said what we were both feeling in that moment of complete openness and vulnerability.

The crowd was pushing Lee and Bob around the room but not before Aaron and I were introduced to their twin girls and were able to have a picture taken with them. They were barely 10 years old and had gone through more than any child should.

The day we arrived in New York, the November 8, 2010 People Magazine had hit the stands with an issue featuring a story on Operation Mend. Aaron was pictured in it, as well as being named one of their *2010 Heroes of the Year.* When we arrived at the airport I had picked up several copies. I brought one to the reception that night. I handed it to Aaron to sign and give to Lee. He quickly put it back in my hands telling me to give it to her, so I did. She was so overwhelmed at receiving a copy; she then had me showing it as others in the room looked on.

Four wounded warriors and Dr. Timothy Miller were featured in this article.

As I mingled through the room, I found myself at a table with four wonderful women. They wanted to ask me personal questions and I told them they could ask me anything. I was completely open to whatever they wanted to know. I shared with them about Aaron's experiences as well as mine and answered all there questions and more. One of the women at this table, I would meet again and would become one of my dearest friends, Tara O'Rourke Howard, who lost her husband to a traumatic brain injury.

As the reception came to a close, there was time for one last picture to be taken. This would become one of my favorite pictures, among many more to come...

As Aaron grabbed my coat, he let Bob know we would not be attending the dinner that followed. Aaron had an interview at the Fox station several blocks away. It was a satellite feed with someone in Chicago. We grabbed a taxi to the studio and were greeted by a production assistant; she helped us with our name tags and through security. Then took us back to where the interview was to take place. The corner set was ready and Aaron took his chair while having a microphone snaked up his jacket. I watched as Aaron answered questions and put everyone at ease with his lite humor. Fifteen minutes later we were on our way back to our hotel.

The next night was the main event for *Stand Up For Heroes.* Aaron guided me around to the various places we were to be at the times we were to be there.

Before we went to The Beacon Theater, we met with a group of wounded warriors who were gathered to attend the event. Lee and Bob would come in for a few minutes, for pictures before heading over.

It was a very cold night in New York City to be standing in line to reach the "Red Carpet." As we got closer to the head of the line, Lee came out of the tent where the press was, and grabbed Aaron. She said Bob would be out to get me in just a minute. I saw Bob come out of the tent and immediately side tract by a reporter, as he looked back toward where I was standing. The lady would not allow me to move toward him and he could not see me. Bob headed back inside as his time was running out. After a few minutes, Aaron reappeared and asked if Bob had come out. I said he wasn't able to reach me so Aaron took me inside the tent.

Aaron was in high demand to have his picture taken with a variety of people and as his "Arm Candy," I was included in several of the pictures.

We would walk the line of photographers with one person, and then be shuffled back to the beginning to start again with another person. It felt like a "Premiere."

As the night of entertainment began with Jon Stewart as the Master of Ceremonies, it just got better and better. Everyone expected to see Bruce Springsteen, but when Tony Bennett stepped on stage there was a hush that fell over the entire audience. We all knew this was a once in a lifetime experience and we would never forget the wonderful voice that belonged to the one and only, Tony Bennett.

Jerry Seinfeld was on stage and had us all laughing and enjoying his talent of putting the everyday things of life into a simple perspective. Bruce Springsteen was the driving force of the auction as he donated his guitar.

As the night came to an end, we were all tired and yet excited by the auction and how much had been raised. We would have an early morning and I was ready for some sleep, as was Aaron.

The next morning, all the wounded warriors and their caregivers were to attend *Good Morning America* with Bob Woodruff. He wanted Aaron in front, so if he had a chance to pull him into the interview he could. Aaron made sure I had a chair to sit in. It had only been three weeks since my last surgery and I was tired. We waited for the show to begin and then Bob's interview about the night before and how much money had been raised.

After the show finished we had a chance to meet some of the members of *Good Morning America*. When Robin Roberts came by, I motioned to her and she knelt down by my chair. I had the opportunity to tell her, "Thank you, for sharing your experience with Breast Cancer with the American people. It gave us all so much courage." She touched my knee, smiled and thanked me then moved on to the next person who wanted a little of her time.

Aaron and I had a plane to catch, we headed to the hotel to change and gather our things. As soon as we boarded the plane a lady grabbed my arm and said, "I saw you on Good Morning America this morning!" I told her yes she had and it was very exciting, then went back to my assigned seat and collapsed.

I couldn't wait to do this again, but the next time I hoped to have my own hair...

It would be 2012 before I would attend another, Stand Up For Heroes, event. I was so sorry to miss the 2011 one, but Aaron had other things on his agenda, for all of us...

The 2012 *Stand Up For Heroes* was even more exciting than the first one I had attended. This was the first time Aaron would speak, and I had been asked to be present for comments during an interview Aaron was doing for *Night Line*.

This year all the caregivers were treated to makeovers covering clothes, hair and makeup. I had so much fun with the people who donated their time to help us pick out outfits to wear. The two men who were helping me were a joy! When we introduced ourselves, I told them to just call me Mom, like everyone else did. They looked at each other and laughed while saying, "That's great, we will." When we got down to shoes, all in my size were just about gone. They assured me, more would arrive the next morning and asked me to come back down then. When I went down the next afternoon, after having my make-up and hair done, I looked through the various rooms for one of the two men. I found them in the second room and went over to where they were helping someone else. They both looked at me and said, "Hi Mom, we have the perfect shoes hidden for you." They received the shipment and told me when they saw these shoes, they grabbed them saying these were for "Mom." They were perfect and I thanked them, as we laughed at the thought of them being *snatched* for me. I had to run up to my room and go to the interview with *Night Line*. When I returned, Aaron checked out my new hairstyle and clothes, he loved my new look.

When doing any interview it can go on for an hour and wind up as a twenty second spot on air. We found out as we were being interviewed, it was going to air that very night after the nightly news. The text messages were flying to family and friends to watch. I hurried back to my room and changed again before the nights activities were to begin.

Once again I was given the opportunity to walk on the Red Carpet with my handsome son, "Cpl. Aaron P. Mankin."

After a few rounds on the Red Carpet, Aaron went to join those who were to be on stage and I went to my seat. Aaron was to speak immediately after Bob and Lee, and the hope was for him to set the tone for the night. He did it well, his stories were captivating and the challenge he issued to every American was bold and filled with truth making me cry as usual. But what really got me, this was the first time I had seen him "Salute" since the IED had done its damage...

After the program, I boarded the bus to return to the hotel before Aaron. He had remained back stage for a few minutes and then came out to get on the bus. As he boarded there was shouting from several of the Marines on board, who had not noticed when I came on. "Where's Mom" was heard, as Aaron took his second step up into the bus. It was so funny, as Aaron started to stammer and look around behind him then searchingly to make sure I was there. When he finally spotted me, Aaron pointed out that I was already on the bus as he came and sat next to me. I felt like the whole Marine Corps was watching out for "Mom."

When we got to the Hotel, I went upstairs to catch the last part of the broadcast. Some of the guys and wives had roamed into the bar to talk about all that had happened during the program. At the top of the list were Roger Waters and the band he had pulled together from Walter Reeds, Music Corps program. They were amazing to say the least. When Marine Timothy Dunley, a double amputee, sang Wide River to Cross, the room exploded…

When I got back upstairs, I turned on the television and searched for the ABC channel to catch *Night Line*. They were just going to commercial and would have the interview up next. I called Aaron on his cell phone to let him know it was on now!

He came crashing into our room just as the program came back on. We watched to see how all the footage had been arranged into the short amount of time to air it. Aaron was great, and showed his humor and his strength while being interviewed, I got in one quote.

I summed it all up with, "They've all earned the gratitude of our nation and our citizens; and like Aaron said, "IF YOU DIDN'T SERVE, SERVE THOSE WHO DID."

Veterans Week 2011

Aaron had been planning for weeks in preparation for the Fifth Annual *IAVA Awards Ceremony,* in New York City. He wanted as many of his family and friends to be there as possible. Aaron's brothers, Jason and Kyle with his son, Henry, along with his cousin Devin Mayes were able to come. Aaron's friends, Travis and Ryan Coursey rounded out the rest of the group. This was his week and he wanted to share it with everyone.

The first night would be the Awards Ceremony. The next morning, we would attend a breakfast at the Governors Home and that evening we would all go to the Dedication at the Memorial where the Twin Towers had been. Several of the Operation Mend group would be there along with Todd, Dana and Ron Katz as well as Dr. Timothy Miller.

All had arrived at the New York Warwick Hotel and gone to their assigned rooms, as we prepared to attend the *IAVA (Iraq Afghanistan Veterans of America)* ceremony that night. Aaron was to receive the 2011 Veterans Leadership Award and Stephen Colbert, the Civilian Service Award.

Before I attended the ceremony I wanted to read the press release first. As I read about Stephen, it described him as the "Bob Hope" of our times. I hadn't known the extent of his commitment to our troops overseas and at home, before this night.

Then the paragraph about Aaron; it told *he was one of our community's single most powerful advocates. His leadership, courage, tenacity and humility had inspired wounded veterans, and countless people around the world. Aaron's story is one of hope and perseverance that all Americans must know about.* This description was so true, and yet so hard for Aaron to accept.

My thoughts went to his question, years before, if I had ever thought he would be, "known." My child was being honored for so much he had given back and he could not comprehend the impact his life had on so many others...

Aaron had a problem with being called a "Hero." He would tell me, all he did for his country was to be blown up. This seemed so minuet when he looked at those who suffered injuries during combat in defending and saving their fellow service members, and those who had suffered more severe wounds than his.

I told Aaron the example he set enduring so many surgeries, his speaking out for Veterans, holding the people of this country accountable for the support of our military families, all these doors he stepped through made him a *"True American Hero."*

How many had said "Stop," after just a few surgeries. But he never said "Stop," to any of it; because this wasn't just for him, it was for all who were still to come. He never gave into the despair, which was constantly within him, to quit and just accept the way things were.

Aaron's "Heroism" came after his injuries in Iraq and the way "One Marine" continued to use his voice to insure others had the same opportunities he did. He started and stayed on a path that had originally thought to take 6-7 months, and is still continuing eight years and more than sixty surgeries later.

Aaron was on stage and presented with the award after a touching introduction and a video outlining his life (now only 29 years old) after the IED explosion. This night, I would hear the words spoken that all around him knew to be true, Aaron said, "Tonight, I fell like one (hero)."

As he was waiting for the standing applause to settle he touched his left ear, as he always did to let me know he loved me...

My heart was filled with so many emotions; I can't begin to put all of them into words. This was a major break thru in the battle that rages inside, the ones which only he can know...

The next morning we were invited to a brunch at the Governors Manson and tour the historical building. Henry really enjoyed the library and all it had to offer and I enjoyed spending time with him.

That night we were scheduled to attend America's Response Memorial Unveiling and Official Dedication Ceremony, at the site where the Twin Towers once stood. This was one of the most moving ceremony's I have ever attended.

The story behind this statue was one of courage and humility, one I had never heard before. Bill White was the driving force behind this statue and the grass roots effort which brought this national treasure to the forefront, in honoring our Armed Forces.

I had never heard of the Special Operations Team of the *Horse Soldier's* until that night. In this picture you can see the magnificent size and presence this statue possesses. It contains a symbol from all branches of our military services, so all are represented. There's also a small piece of metal, from The Towers, in its base to complete the story it tells. Behind the statue can be seen the steps that once lead to the Twin Towers, where our countrymen bled and died during this attack on our nation. I wept at the vision as I remembered...

The statue is one that represents those who lead the invasion into Afghanistan in the months that followed the attack on our nation. The *"Horse Soldiers"* helped to defeat the Taliban and push back the Al Qaeda militants into the mountains of Pakistan. They rode in on horseback to speak with local tribal warlords to gain military support. There were those among them, who gave the ultimate sacrifice in securing an early victory which many did not think achievable in just a few weeks, not months or years.

Those who served would be referred to as the *"Quiet Professionals"* who would never seek out credit or recognition. They would insist this memorial represent all those who had served and sacrificed

in Iraq and Afghanistan, as well as all wars. Vice President, Joe Biden, was the night's guest speaker. After the ceremonies had concluded,

Aaron and I, among others, had the opportunity to meet him. Aaron and I are standing with our backs to the camera in this photo.

When I was introduced by Aaron as his mother, the Vice President gave me a hug and kissed my cheek. He was very gracious to one of the other mother's and I, he told us if we ever needed help for our son's to call, and we would be put through on his private line.

We were not allowed to leave the building until the Vice President had left. The Secret Service agent wouldn't even let Jason go into the restroom while everyone was waiting for him to clear the building. When we were finally allowed to leave, there was a humble and quite spirit in the night air. Ryan came up beside me and took my arm as the rest of our crowd walked back to the bus. I thanked him for his steady comfort and he replied, "Anytime Momma."

This was a very good week…

The following morning Aaron would be in the Veteran's Day Parade along with the others from Operation Mend. It was a cold morning on the streets of New York City, so Jason and I watched the parade from the warmth of our hotel room.

That afternoon we all headed for the airport and home…

Dinner with the Secretary of Defense

In early January 2012, I received an email from Rene' Bardorf. I met her when she was working for the *Bob Woodruff Foundation* at the *Stand Up For Heroes* event in 2010. Aaron had met her a couple of years before I did. Rene' was now working as the Deputy Asst. Secretary of Defense for Community and Public Outreach. Her email was requesting Aaron and me to attend a dinner with The Secretary of Defense, Leon Panetta.

This was followed by an email from Lt. Col. Damien Pickart, who worked directly with Rene'. We would talk often in making the arrangements for this dinner and other opportunities in the near future. I admired him and his professionalism; it was obvious to see how much he enjoyed his work.

The purpose of this dinner was a little vague, but my understanding was that all The Secretary wanted to do was just talk to some of the wounded warriors and their caregivers to gain some insight as to the experiences of each.

I received the email, because they were having trouble getting through to Aaron. He was going through one of his shut down episodes and wouldn't respond to any emails, texts or phone calls.

Aaron would not return my calls or messages either. I felt this was an important opportunity and was determined for Aaron to attend and voice his experiences to the Secretary of Defense. So, I continued to answer messages on Aaron's behalf and make the arrangements for us to attend.

While I was finishing up the arrangements and gathering the information about the dinner, Aaron called. I got him up-to-speed and now he was on board. We would continue with the flight arrangements and timing between the two of us.

The official invitation came with a list of those who would be attending. As I was looking at the list I was pleased to see Debbie and her son Steven Shultz on the list. There would be twelve wounded warriors and nine caregivers; some fathers other mothers and a sister and wife. There was a full range of people attending that would represent all aspects of the wounded warrior experience.

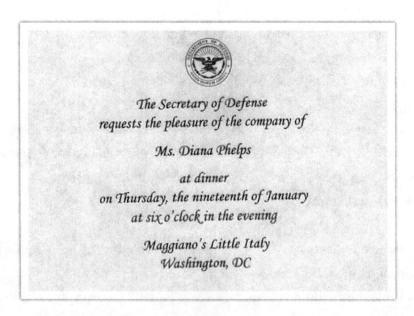

The Secretary of Defense
requests the pleasure of the company of

Ms. Diana Phelps

at dinner
on Thursday, the nineteenth of January
at six o'clock in the evening

Maggiano's Little Italy
Washington, DC

It would be a quick trip. Aaron and I would fly in on Thursday and had been told to be prepared to go straight to the restaurant. Our luggage would be taken from the airport to the hotel and we would be met and escorted to where the dinner would be. From there, we would go to the hotel and fly back home the next morning. We would be escorted through every step of this trip.

All those who had been invited had arrived at Maggiano's Little Italy and taken to a private room on the second floor. We were all getting to know each other over drinks and hors d'oeuvres while we waited for the Secretary to arrive. The servers began to bring in our dinner, so we all took our places around the outside of the U shaped table. The other staff members suggested we go ahead and start eating while we were waiting.

The Secretary of Defense, Leon Panetta arrived just as we were taking our first bits of dinner and laughed at us for starting without him. He was followed into the closed room by several security men. I hadn't really thought about the security issues surrounding this meeting, until then. I realized the short notice; the plans surrounding our arrival and the transport to the restaurant were all a part of national security.

When everyone was seated again, Leon Panetta took a seat in the middle of the U shaped table. Coming right to the point, he asked each to tell their story as he went around the room. He listened intently, with compassion on his face to each story and wrote in his little pocket tablet from time to time.

Aaron was seated next to last in the order of the table. We were both surprised at how young most of the others were. Some were injured just months before this night. When Aaron finished speaking, all I had to say was there had not been a Reconstructive Surgeon on staff at BAMC for the two years Aaron was there. This got an immediate response, as Leon Panetta looked disturbingly at Aaron. Aaron nodded his head and was told, "This will be taken care of, and I promise you that!" After all had told their stories, Leon Panetta spoke of change and how important our input had been. We finished dinner and everyone mingled around the room, as we now knew each other so much better. The "Coins" we each received from The Secretary, would be a reminder of the honor we were given to share the common stories of all veterans and perhaps we made a difference that night...

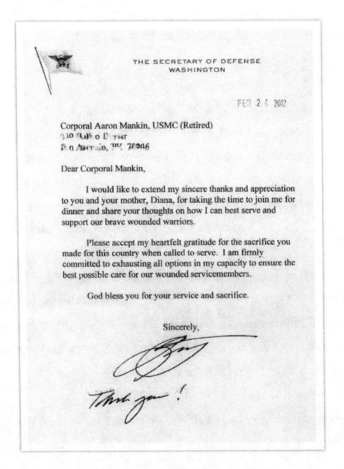

THE SECRETARY OF DEFENSE
WASHINGTON

FEB 2 4 2012

Corporal Aaron Mankin, USMC (Retired)

Dear Corporal Mankin,

    I would like to extend my sincere thanks and appreciation to you and your mother, Diana, for taking the time to join me for dinner and share your thoughts on how I can best serve and support our brave wounded warriors.

    Please accept my heartfelt gratitude for the sacrifice you made for this country when called to serve. I am firmly committed to exhausting all options in my capacity to ensure the best possible care for our wounded servicemembers.

    God bless you for your service and sacrifice.

Sincerely,

Thank you!

We were taken back to the Hotel where our luggage was and checked into our rooms. When Aaron and I got to our room we opened the curtains to look at the Washington D.C. skyline. There was a structure neither one of us could figure out what it was. I had called down to the desk requesting more pillows and when the man brought them, Aaron asked about what we were seeing. He explained it was a monument near the Pentagon which had been donated by the Air Force, in remembrance of 9/11. The shape depicted the path of the first jets lifting off that day, to defend our nation.

The following morning we were able to have breakfast with Rene' and Lt. Col. Damien Pickart and visit with them both. Rene' brought her two children and it was a time for remembering and relaxing with old and new friends.

Lt. Col. Damien Pickart stood next to Aaron and Deputy Asst. Secretary of Defense, Rene' Bardorf stood with Steven after breakfast while Debbie Shultz and I took pictures. Then we were off to the airport.

After we returned, Aaron went back into "seclusion" again. He was still living in San Antonio which was a 7½ drive from my door to his. When he wouldn't answer my calls and messages there wasn't much I could do except wait or drive...

The effects of PTSD and the personal struggles were overwhelming him. Aaron had custody of his two young children and all he wanted was to stay in his house and just do what had to be done.

A couple of weeks after the dinner meeting, I received another email from Rene'. Aaron would not respond to me or anyone else, his message box was full and wouldn't accept anymore. Once again, I did all the arranging for the possibility of what was being offered to us both.

Subject: Trying to reach you for a special opportunity

Aaron, Diana,

We'd like to share with the two of you another very special opportunity.

If you're not aware, the President plans to host a formal dinner at the White House the evening of Wednesday, Feb. 29, to thank those who served and sacrificed in the nearly nine-year conflict in Iraq. While hundreds of thousands served honorably, only 200 will be able to attend the dinner.

Ms. Bardorf would like to nominate you both. What we are in need of - in very short order - is some personal information: your full name with middle initial, social security numbers and dates of birth. The purpose of this information is to allow US Secret Service to conduct a background check on those nominated to attend before the White House staff begins vetting and cutting the list down to 200.

While there are no guarantees on who will ultimately get selected, we feel very strongly that Aaron would well represent the tens of thousands of wounded service members from OIF.

Please let us know at your earliest convenience if you are able to accept this unique honor.

Best regards,
Rene'

We would not be notified, if we were selected, until a few days before the Formal Dinner. Aaron and I had to be checked out by the Secret Service and had to have our documents in order. Aaron still had not responded to my calls when Rene' inquired if Aaron was willing to accept this invitation. I assured her, he was.

The next email confirmed our acceptance and invitation to attend this historical event.

Aaron, Diana

I'm pleased to announce that the two of you have been selected to attend the formal OIF dinner at the White House next Wednesday evening, Feb. 29.

I called and left a voice mail with you both, but from your previous email response to Ms. Bardorf, it appears and you are both available and excited to attend the event. I will provide further details (attire, travel, etc) in the coming days, but what needs to take place soonest is confirming your attendance with an RSVP to the White House social office either through telephone or email:

2⁓ ⋅ ⋈⋅ ⁿ ↑ ⋅ (Select Option 2)

Sᴀᴅs. ᵃⁿ᷈ ⱼ ℘ ⋈⟨ꞵ℮ᵇ↓ch

I will continue to try and reach you through close of business today. If I haven't heard back, I will RSVP on your behalf before I depart for the evening.

Best regards,

Damien

Lt Col Damien Pickart
Staff Officer
Community & Public Outreach
Office of the Assistant Secretary of Defense Public Affairs

I did RSVP immediately for Aaron as well as myself, even though I still could not get any response from him.

Four days before we were to fly out, the Press landed on Aaron's doorstep. The announcement from the White House of the guest list had been released and he and I were on it. I received a call from him that night and the first statement when I answered was, "Will, I guess we're going to the White House."

Aaron didn't sound too excited about going, but as the arrangements were being finalized he realized what a privilege and honor this opportunity was.

The White House

A Nation's Gratitude

On February 10th, this letter was sent from the White House along with the names of those who would be attending the dinner called, "A Nation's Gratitude."

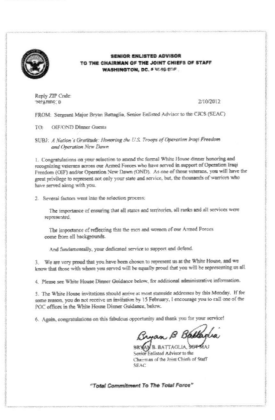

I received an e-mail on the 10th; confirming Aaron and I had been chosen to attend the formal White House dinner. There would be seventy-eight service members altogether.

Aaron and I would receive several e-mails giving us information including the proper attire for this formal affair. I enjoyed the pictures of the different uniforms and how they should be worn. It was a by-service chart showing the authorized uniforms.

Those of us, who were attending as guests, were instructed on our attire as well. I know this may sound trivial to some, but the importance of being included with this group of Heroes and the opportunity to go to the White House should never be taken lightly, no matter what your political views are. The history these walls have seen can only be imagined.

Celebrating the end of a war with a formal White House dinner was a first for any presidential administration and many opposed it. Some of those who fought in Iraq were still fighting in Afghanistan and we are all waiting for the day we can have a parade to celebrate all returning veterans.

The agenda was set and excitement filled the air as we began this adventure into one of the most treasured, historical places in this country. We all had our instructions and times on where to be when. The security issues were firmly in place and we knew what was expected of us.

Before we were allowed to enter the reception, we were required to provide a picture I.D. and our names had to be on their check list. The person responsible for the security checks and getting us to the White House was Sgt. Maj. Bryan Battaglia, the senior Enlisted Advisor to the Chairman of the Joint Chiefs of Staff.

It didn't take long before Bryan and Aaron were talking and laughing as though they had been brothers growing up together.

Bryan would tell me, when Aaron wasn't within hearing distance, how much he appreciated the sacrifice he had made for this country. It was a good thing Bryan had a broad chest to hold all those medals. He earned every one of them and I appreciate all that he has done for my Freedom.

Aaron had been approached by the Today Show people for an interview, before the reception, and then to follow us around the room posing us with other guests. About 20 minutes before the first security check, Aaron sat with them and answered questions with his usual flare. I loved watching him turn these interviews into a game of wits, while answering with humor that only he could get away with.

During the reception the photographer who was following Aaron and me around the room, would place us in certain positions for a photo. I was so happy to see Debbie and Steven Shultz at this event. Steven had just received a Seeing Eye dog and we all fell in love with Sonny. But, he was on duty so we were careful not to get in the way of the training they had both gone through.

The press would only be allowed to attend the Hotel reception during the afternoon; this would last for one hour and fifteen minutes. Next, we would board secured buses and be escorted by a motorcade to the White House. Before we left for the White House, the rain began and the staff members were scrambling to get enough umbrellas for all of us.

The buses were outside with the police escorts waiting for us to board. Without incident, we were all boarded and on our way to the White House. Now that the press was gone, the excitement began to bubble up inside me along with the naturally intense nervousness when meeting a President; this would be my fourth to meet.

When we got to the White House we had to go through security in single file. The line was stretched out to the street as the rain fell and needless to say my hair was doing its own thing. When I reached the security area it reminded me of an airport, except for the dogs. Before entering, the final step was to stand alone next to a couple of German Shepard dogs, who were behind a wooden gate. If they didn't respond then you passed the inspection.

Now, Aaron and I could enter and explore the White House and as much history as we could take in. We were told we could take all the pictures we wanted and the lack of corded off areas and secret service, gave us a sense of freedom to roam. The first thing we saw was the White House orchestra. (That's their official name.)

Their music was soft and soothing. All the lighting in the rooms had been dimmed. There was a yellow cast in each room that made it appear the only lighting was coming from candles, as it did when it was first built. The rooms were much smaller and the ceilings much higher than I had imagined. I loved the fireplaces in each room, realizing they were the only heat when these rooms were built.

The first room we entered was the Red Room. The walls were covered with a satin like material which gave the room a very rich and warm feel. There were a number of portraits on the walls. I was impressed at the size of these portraits and the way they were placed on the walls. They were placed two and sometimes three high, from just above the floor to the ceiling. The frames were magnificent in their antique glory. The furnishings were just as impressive.

I love antique furnishings and enjoyed looking at the chairs and various tables in all the rooms, Just as I was about to take a picture of the Green room, Aaron came rushing by to capture a picture of something that had caught his eye. There was just so much to see we found ourselves running from one room to another.

Next we noticed the bust of President Lincoln and decided to do one of our goofy face poses. I was expecting some security person to come running toward us as I was about to plant a big red kiss on this white, marble treasure. The picture was taken without incident.

Aaron just can't take me anywhere!

It's as if President Kennedy is looking down at the young marine standing there, as Aaron posed in the yellowish glow of the room.

The place I wanted to see next was the "Lady's Room," or I should say rooms. The first was a parlor, with the portraits of many of the most famous First Ladies. A very comfortable place to sit and visit before joining the men folk.

The second room was the "Powder Room." The tables and mirrors provided many women a comfortable place for fixing their attire or makeup and hair. Off to the right, where the restroom stalls and sink area.

When I saw how spectacular the main parlor was I came out into the hall to tell Aaron. He walked right in and started taking pictures. The few ladies who were in there just looked at him, but none said one word. Aaron didn't venture past the parlor so no one was offended.

The next thing we knew some of the staff were asking us to move toward the main reception hall as they began to close off one room at a time. The President and First Lady would be greeting everyone soon.

Aaron and I were standing in the back of the room waiting for Bob Woodruff to come in. He was down stairs with the President doing an interview. As we stood there, I had my back to the doors and was facing Aaron while we talked. Everyone in the room had begun to form a line to go into the next room and be presented to the President and First Lady.

Just before Bob came in Vice President, Joe Biden came up behind me and gave me a hug and kiss on the cheek as he said, "Hi Mom." We had met a couple of months earlier and he still remembered me as "Mom." Bob came rushing in and suddenly realized he was standing in front of the Vice President. Aaron and Bob were standing at attention as the V.P. stood there, with his arm around my shoulder, and began to speak very strongly to both of them.

Joe Biden told them they both must hear what he had to say and he had to say it. "The bad days will never go away. But they will come less and less frequent, as time goes by. You get a calendar and mark those bad days, every time they come. Pretty soon you will begin to see how the good days last longer and the bad days are shorter. But, don't ever expect them to go away completely."

In the midst of this story, I watched as Aaron's eyes began to water, but not a drop fell. Bob hung his head at one point and I thought I saw a tear fall and quickly wiped away before he looked back up. The Vice President was then called to join the others and excused himself. At that moment, I believed it was for that purpose God had placed us in that room. They both needed to hear those words, from a man who had lost his wife and two of his three young children in a car accident many years ago. He knew tragedy...

The line to the President was beginning to shorten and as we stood there talking one of the staff members came over and asked us to please get in line. Bob and Aaron had become such close friends over the years and truly enjoyed each other.

As we headed toward the other end of the room, Bob turned and said he felt as though he didn't belong at this dinner because he wasn't in the military. I hushed him, telling him that he had put his life on the line and he had been injured while doing the same job Aaron did. I wasn't going to hear any more about it, from this man who had been through and done so much.

Aaron and I were the last to go through the line and I stood back for a few seconds, so he could have a moment for himself. Then he held his hand out to me and introduced me as his mother to President

Obama. He took my hand and said, "Oh Mom, mothers get a hug," as he swept me up and hugged me and kissed my cheek. He then introduced me to the First Lady.

After all the proper things were said of gratitude, I started to tell a story. I told them it was Aaron's great-grandmother's twenty-fifth birthday. The President looked puzzled for a moment then caught on this was the 29th of February, leap year. She would have been 100. So in remembrance of her, I had worn some of her jewelry to the White House. The First Lady was impressed with the jewelry and was admiring the bracelet, choker and earrings as she asked the photographers to come in closer. The President swept me up again, and gave me another hug. The First Lady continued to hold my hand until we were at arm's length. I turned and looked into her eyes saying, "I'm so proud of you for being such a strong woman." She replied, "Oh no, I'm proud of you, for the strong woman you are." She then gave my hand a tug and let go.

The staff was eagerly pushing us to take our seats in the next room, where the state dinners were held. Aaron and I found our tables, with the menu and place cards with the White House emblem.

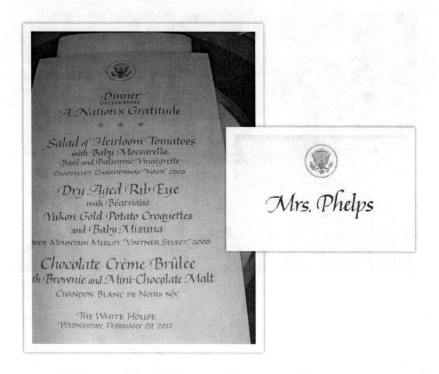

The dining room was exquisite. As was the meal and those we shared it with.

As the night came to an end, we toasted to all who could not be there that night...

While I Traveled

On the plane from Washington D.C. back home, for the second time in little more than a month, I began to think of all the trips I had taken over the past few years and of the people whom I had shared some of my stories with.

I have met so many interesting people in airports and on airplanes. When I travel, it is to meet up with Aaron for a surgery or one of his speaking engagements. I'm usually a little nervous and have found talking and telling my stories is a way to release the tension that builds up inside me. I will strike up a conversation with just about anyone I come into contact with.

The ticketing agents, security people at the check points, attendants at the airline desks, the people sitting by me waiting to board, the crew members who greet me at the door of the plane, the person seated next to me, all would become my captive audiences.

On one occasion while going through security, I was fumbling with my driver's license, boarding pass, purse and carry-on bag. The bag I was using was a small, red one with wheels and an extended handle. As I tried to get it to stand on its own, the handle fell and landed at the feet of the Security Officer who was guarding the check point. On the back of my bag was a sticker with the Marine Corps emblem. He asked, as he was picking up the handle, "Who's the Marine?" I told him my son, and shared a little of Aaron's story as I was handing my ID over to the women at the podium. As I finished and thanked him for retrieving my bag, he held out his hand to me and as I took it he slipped a "Coin" to me. With a crack in his voice, he simply said, "I want you to have this." He turned quickly away, not wanting me to see the emotion on his face and before I had a chance to respond.

When I had a chance to look at what he had given me, I realized what a special "gift" this was. The coin was one that had obviously been carried in this man's pocket for a long time. It had the marks of being handled and held on to, as a constant reminder of years gone by and friends never forgotten. For him to have parted with this piece of himself will always be a reminder to me of the bond between brothers of war. I carry it with me constantly, as he did…

A VETERAN
is a person who wrote
a blank check payable to the
United States of America
for an amount of
up to and including
one's life.

While flying home after one of Aaron's surgeries, I was sitting in an airport waiting for my connection. I had been talking to the lady behind the counter about the flight; I guess she could see how tired I was. After I was seated, she came over to where I was and knelt down beside me to speak. She said, The Lord told her to come over and give me her phone numbers. She went on to say if I ever need to go anywhere, or needed to get to my son, to just call one of the numbers on the piece of paper she had given me. She continued to explain, as an employee she could fly for free and wanted to give me those miles. It was what God wanted her to do. She said she had never done such a thing before, but it was the right thing to do...

I met one young woman who was worried about Breast Cancer. She had just been diagnosed and was uncertain of what the future would hold for her. Because I had been through the whole ordeal, I was able to talk to her in a way no one else could. She listened intently and asked questions as I witnessed to her of the miracle that had taken place in my life and how all evidence of cancer had been erased. After we spoke and began to board the plane, she turned to me and thanked me for sharing with her. She said her whole outlook on her situation had changed and her fear was gone...

One time, when I got on a plane headed back to Oklahoma City, I took my seat next to a man sitting by the window. He appeared to be a military man even though he was in civilian clothes. We began to talk and he knew who Aaron was. He had read some articles about Aaron and seen him speak on some Internet features. It turned out he was in the Air Force and stationed at Tinker Air Force Base in Oklahoma City. He didn't mention his rank, but apparently he was rather high in the chain of command. I gathered this from one of the experiences he told me about.

This Airman was assigned to a mission someplace in South America. He was to be dropped off in the middle of the jungle near an encampment of Marines. They would be helping him carry out the mission. One thing he kept saying was, "I love my Marines because I know they will keep me alive."

When he parachuted into the jungle the Marines were quick to pick him up and take him to their camp. He asked where he could change clothes and get into his camouflage wear. One of the Marines directed him to a small tent and told him the clothes were inside. They all gathered around after he went into the tent, waiting for the show to begin. It was soon apparent; the clothes he was putting on had been intentionally infested with fire ants. After a minute or so he came running, jumping, hooting and hollering trying to strip out of the clothes he barely had on. He had been initiated into the group; he still loves his Marines, much to their amusement.

One young man had just finished Marine boot camp and was headed home for a short visit. He seemed a little nervous about what lay before him when he was deployed. I tried to assure him that whatever was going to be would be, as long as he stayed close to his Maker and remembered his training. I told him to enjoy his family as if it were the last time he would see them and to live the rest of his life the same way. We are not promised any tomorrows so take care of things today.

He gave me a shy grin, nodded his head as he said, "Yes Mom," and walked off the plane. I wonder where he is today...

When on a plane to Washington D.C. I sat next to a woman who was rather quiet, but as we began to talk she became quite interested in my stories. After talking for a while, I told her I was going to write a book about everything that had happened with Aaron, from a mother's point of view. She asked me if I knew how to write a book and I told her no, I didn't have a clue all I knew was how to share my stories. Then Allison Silbergerg told me, she was a writer and had a book out, "Visionaries in Our Midst."

Photo by, Karen Elliott Greisdorf

She was very encouraging and agreed I should write this book. A couple of months later we exchanged messages, she told me to write the book just like I was sitting next to her on the plane. Just tell my stories, they were captivating and empowering to those families who were going through the same things I had gone through. So, I took her advice and began seriously organizing and outlining what purpose I wanted this book to serve.

There are so many others whom I have reached out to and who have touched me during my travels, but filling these pages with more stories would be redundant. So, I'll leave the memories to those I spoke to and hope I touched them in a positive way. I hope I was there at precisely the right moment in time to speak a word or touch your hand as to comfort and change your perception of this world. I believe all of our paths crossed for a reason and "Hope" will spring from that…

I had been talking about writing this book with Aaron for years as I continued to gather material and pictures, from the first phone call through every step of this journey. A couple of years ago Aaron came up with the title for this book, as well as an email address *always a marine mom*, which is who I have become.

When I think of all the wounded young men and women, who come home to be cared for, there are an uncountable number of family, friends and communities who are forever changed…

These are the people I hope to help, by sharing a part of me…

So There I Was

"So there I was." This is a phrase which always gets the attention of all who are listening. Aaron always makes lite of the people who begin a story with this line. He will stop the person who has just uttered these words and gather more people around to listen. He explains when someone starts with the phrase "So there I was," you can always expect to hear a very interesting story.

Now here I am, trying to find the words to express the emotions which have brought me through these last eight years. It has been a journey which has taken me from one end, to the extreme other on the scale of a mother's emotions.

Aaron spoke at an event where he was honored by his home town. As I listened to him speak, I finally heard the words and saw the emotions I had been waiting years for. Within his speech was a release I don't think he even realized was happening, until it was upon him. "I am finally beginning my recovery," was the most important thing to be heard that night, though few comprehended the full meaning of it. The recovery Aaron was speaking of had to do with his battle against PTSD, not the healing of the wounds on the outside of his body.

Six months before this night, a transformation had taken place with the help of friends and family. All of us around Aaron knew it would take moving away from San Antonio, and back home to Rogers, Arkansas, before he could find the support system he so desperately needed.

One weekend in early August, the move had to be made in order to enroll Aaron's daughter in kindergarten at the same school where he had gone. He had been talking about the move for years, but the thought of all to be done was extremely overwhelming for him. Aaron couldn't begin to put the pieces together, the enormity of it all flooding his mind and causing him to "shut down," and accomplish little if anything.

Finally, with the help of so many friends and family, the time had come. Aaron's friends were on their way to move him to Rogers. A couple of weeks earlier he leased the condo which he would make into a new home and a new life for his children, as well as himself.

The morning Aaron arrived in Rogers, he and his friends had been packing and driving for nearly 48 hours, and yet the overwhelming burden had finally been overcome!!!

There was still much to be done and after we enjoyed a good breakfast together, Aaron and I had time to sit and talk while he relaxed. He was so excited; the rest he needed had not yet overcome him. He was pacing around while he told funny stories about the moving and driving, then he stopped and looked at me as he put his hands on my shoulders and said, "Mom, I feel like an enormous boulder has been lifted off my shoulders."

While the next few months past and they all began to settle in, Aaron continued to speak at various events or have another surgery. He took on fewer engagements because the children's schedules were more important. Most times, I would drive over with Jason and fly out with Aaron, leaving Jason to be "Mr. Mom" while we were gone. Maddie and Hunter loved having their uncle around to play with and take care of them, and Jason loved the opportunity to spend time with them.

The difficulty of being a single parent was beginning to sink in with both children having their separate schedules and routines. Aaron wanted to be involved in as many of their school activities as possible. I'm so proud of the parent he has become. The need to support his family was becoming a reality, one which had to be dealt with and planned for as a part of his life. This was not only essential for their future, but to the continuing process of dealing with Aaron's PTSD.

Now, with Aaron back in Rogers it was impossible for him to hide from everyone when he was having a difficult time. In San Antonio, it was just too easy to not answer phone calls and emails for weeks at a time. Aaron was within reach now, and I will not let go of him, no matter what...

Aaron is a grown man, single father of two small children, nationally known public speaker and a medically retired Marine who will always have to deal with the effects of war. He has come to accept the scars he wears as badges of honor. But, those hidden scars are the nightmares he will deal with, in one form or another, for the rest of his life.

As Aaron has the opportunities to speak, each one helps to heal his spirit and soul. With all who suffer from PTSD, they must find a purpose which is more than they are. Aaron found his purpose, in speaking out on behalf of other veterans. I have learned more about his experiences in Iraq from speeches, than I ever have from our conversations.

I became a "Marine Mom," from an ignorant civilian, with the signing of a paper. For every person who enlists, so does their family. Everything from that point on will affect the family and friends who are watching and praying with every move which takes place in the life of their service member.

When Aaron was wounded, the Marine families around me were the ones I depended on the most. I had so much to learn in a matter of days and continue to learn as the years pass. One thing stands out above all else, I will always be a Marine Mom, and am proud to be one!!!

For every wounded warrior there is a multitude of family, friends and communities, who are forever changed. The affairs of our heroes are a reflection on our society and how we are gauged by others. We are judged on our morality as to how we support, not just our heroes, but their families as well.

With everything we have gone through together, Aaron has taught me so much about myself. He has shown me, through example and encouragement, I can accomplish anything. The choice is mine, to be as much or as little as I want, and Aaron will be right there beside me all the way, and I by his.

Acknowledgments

During the two years while I have been putting the pieces of this book together, I have put it down many times and decided it was an impossible task. I would go for weeks without entering my office or going through the mountain of pictures and research overflowing in it. As time would go by, I would always come back to the original concept of why this story must be told.

As difficult as it has been to put down all the events I have lived through, I came to realize how important it is to share them with those who are in the midst of their own life changing events. I have been overwhelmed by the enormous number of people who are trying to find their way through their own personal tragedies.

Without the constant encouragement from my family, this book would never have been completed. The patience and understanding of my husband, Don has been remarkable, allowing me to work at all hours of the day and night when the inspiration would be so strong to write. Even when other household matters needed to be done, he would pick up the slack. Then watching quietly giving me space and time, as I would withdraw within myself as the realities of what I was writing would bring painful memories back.

There have been so many people who have encouraged me along the way, please forgive me if I don't mention each and every one of you. It does not make you any less important in the process of the completion of this book.

To my son, Cpl. Aaron P. Mankin, through his courage and fortitude in dealing with the circumstances of his life's journey, has given me the strength to put all this on paper along with his encouragement and editing skills in the completion of these written words.

To my other two children, Sarah and Jason, and family members who have often been put on the back burner while I was concentrating on this project. I have to say their needs were even neglected at times, while I would be researching and gathering information and the many times I would be away with Aaron. I must thank them for listening to my constant questions and requests for their opinions while I wrote story after story. They are "Heroes" to me!

I will be forever in debt to all the doctors, nurses and medical persons who give, each and every day, back to the wounded warriors with all they have.

To Ron and Maddie Katz, for their vision and willingness to give back the humanity the ravages of war have taken from our nations heroes. Through these two passionate people was born a new and innovative concept, now known as "Operation Mend."

To Dr. Timothy Miller, for his masterful surgical skills and unwavering dedication to the challenge brought before him, a mere THANK YOU is not even close.

As for all the special friends associated with Operation Mend, I cannot find the words to describe the emotions within me for all you have done for Aaron and me, as well as all the other heroes. You are all remarkably talented and generous people.

I could not have gotten through all the ups and downs that would be thrown our way without the love and support of our "Buddy Family," Todd and Dana Katz, Hailey, Gracen, Sara, Sean, Dusty, Oreo, Kady, Bella and all their extended families. All of them as well as Ron and Maddie, will always be "My Family."

I must thank Allison Silbergerg for giving me the concept of writing this book as if I were sitting next to her, just telling my stories and her advice along the way.

To my childhood best friend, Elaine Johnson Byrd, I am so thankful for her love and the way she continually makes me feel like I can do anything.

Without the comfort of the "Quilting Community" throughout this country the lives of my family and all the families of our wounded warriors would be so much less. Your "Art" has held us in moments of crises and truly brought comfort to us all.

To Melanie Hanson Davis and Love Your Veterans for their encouragement, guidance, cherished friendships and the opportunities to share my stories in a variety of platforms, I am humbled.

And last but most important, to our countries Heroes, their families and friends, who have helped pick up our wounded, cared for them and given them hope. So many of you have created organizations that provide services and support, where there was none before. Because you saw the need and acted on it, you have my complete admiration and undying gratitude.

CPSIA information can be obtained at www.ICGtesting.com
Printed in the USA
LVOW12*1430180913

353039LV00019B/66/P